He must increase

Chelsey is that friend who will walk beside you and help you embrace what it means to live fully in the power of God's love, grace, wisdom, peace, and hope. Each page is filled with biblical truths that will shift the lens through which you see your life and equip you with the tools you need to hear God's voice so you can willingly lay down your desires and needs and courageously choose God's plans and purposes.

Wendy Blight, Proverbs 31 Ministries Author

More of Him, Less of Me is a timely devotional written with the intent of moving the reader Godward. It is overflowing with hard-hitting nuggets of biblical truth beautifully balanced by Chelsey's personalized messages of grace. It convicts the heart while softening it, urging the reader to say goodbye to areas of complacency and see the world as Jesus does through the life-changing lens of love. Guaranteed, you will not walk away from this book unchanged.

Anne-Renee Gumley, coauthor of Shiny Things: Mothering on Purpose in a World of Distractions, and co-host of All the Mom Things Podcast

We all need a friend who is running hard after Jesus. Chelsey is that friend and this book is your invitation to run beside her with purpose and passion. Rooted deeply in scripture, these devotions will spur your steps and impact your course as you consider what it means to become more like Jesus in a me-centered world. Get ready to be changed, challenged, and shaped by the One who made you for more.

Alicia Bruxvoort, member of the Proverbs 31 Ministries Writing Team

In a world saturated with self, this devotional is like a breath of fresh air. Chelsey's words will stir your affection for Christ and wrap you in the truth that Jesus is, and always will be, the greatest treasure of all.

Elle Cardel, Founder of Daughter of Delight Ministries

I truly enjoyed this devotional. The scriptures and quotes brought in from others to the insight and stories, it made it so practical and helpful. I can see *More of Him, Less of Me* meeting women wherever they are every day. It prompts you to soak in God's Word and end in prayer for reflection and response to what God is saying. What a gift for communicating God's Word!

Katie Walters, Founder and CEO of Francis & Benedict

Chelsey DeMatteis is an expert on helping us to live with less of the things keeping us from God's best. As a guest on her Living with Less Podcast, I sensed her intense passion for people to encounter God's Word and know His heart. In the same way, *More of Him, Less of Me*, shares personal experiences and Scriptural truths drawing us into a deeper, more meaningful relationship with Jesus. Each devotion reveals God's character and inspires us to stop spinning and start centering our worth on Him.

Angela Donadio, Author and Speaker, Founder of Voice of the Voiceless

I absolutely cherished my early mornings with hot coffee in hand and *More of Him, Less of Me* devotional! Chelsey has done an amazing job in making scripture come alive and making it applicable for my chaotic life. If you desire to feel the Holy Spirit regularly, then you will love this devotional.

Suzanne Mayernick, Founder of Love One International

MORE
OF HIM

less of me

MORE
OF HIM
less of me

Living a Christ-Centered Life
in a Me-Centered World

CHELSEY DEMATTEIS

Arabelle Publishing, LLC
Chesterfield, VA

copyright

More of Him, Less of Me
Living a Christ-centered Life in a Me-centered World
Copyright ©2021 Chelsey DeMatteis

All rights reserved. No part of this book may be reproduced
without prior written permission of the publisher,
except where noted in the text and in the case of brief
quotations embodied in critical articles and reviews.
Request permission through our website.

Published by Arabelle Publishing, LLC
PO Box 2841
Chesterfield, VA 23832
www.arabellebooks.com
IG: @arabellepublishing
IG: @arabellebooks

Unless otherwise indicated, Scripture quotations are from the ESV® Bible
(The Holy Bible, English Standard Version®), copyright © 2001 by Crossway
Bibles, a publishing ministry of Good News Publishers. Used by permission.
All rights reserved.

Credits:
Cover and Interior Design by Julie Basinski

Library of Congress Number: 2021947229
Subjects: Religion, Christian Living, Devotional
ISBN: 9781735632841

Group Sales:
Books are available with special quantity discounts when
purchased in bulk directly from the publisher. This discount
applies to corporations, organizations, and special interest groups.
For more information, email the publisher at
arabellepublishing@gmail.com

This devotional is dedicated to the woman
[whom I never learned her name]
I met on the side of the road
in Akron, OH, in 2011.

TO MY "SISTER IN CHRIST"
The world stood still the moment you approached the
rebellious 19-year-old me, standing with a wrecked car
that perfectly matched my wrecked soul.

You sat with me, looked deep in my eyes, and asked me a
question that would change my life forever.

"HAS ANYONE TOLD YOU THEY LOVE YOU TODAY?"

You were asking something much deeper than what I replied with.
Your next statement opened up places in my heart I didn't know existed.

"God loves you every day. If you need anything just call."

Then you turned around, walked away, and were gone.

I KNOW HE SENT YOU.
HE SENT YOU TO
MEET ME AT MY WELL.

table of CONTENTS

table of
CONTENTS

foreword

I've had a love-hate relationship
with women's devotionals for
as long as I can remember.

In a world that is so self-focused and saturated in sin, it's more than easy to fall into the "feel-good faith" resources crowding the shelves of bookstores across the globe.

For years, I bought those resources and devoured their pep talks. I loved the sugar-coated, quick-fix-filled words that left out anything related to my sin nature and my desperate need for Christ Jesus, my Savior and King.

One day, however, the Lord opened my eyes to the false messages I had made a bad habit out of consuming. These messages not only pointed me away from Him, but they had instilled a false sense of pride within my heart as well.

A pride that believed my need for God was up to me.

A pride that convinced me my need for the truths found in God's Word could be summed up by relying on others.

A pride that deceived me from the truth that it is only because of His strength in me that I can do anything.

In His tender mercy and grace, the Lord looked down on me and rescued me from this path. It is truly only because of His kindness and love that this pride did not devour me. God rescued me in order to set me on the path that leads to His loving embrace.

When my dear friend Chelsey asked me to read this devotional, I was thrilled. Not only did the title she had selected immediately set the tone for what to expect, but it's also the anthem of her heart.

For as long as I have known her, Chelsey has been on a mission to grow the Kingdom of God and make His name known.

The words that fill these pages are not motivational speeches, but rather exactly what we need: a celebration and application of the Gospel's power in our lives, thus encouraging us to live for the glory of God and God alone. My friend Chelsey's stories and reflections on God's Word will help tether your heart to Christ. The next 52 weeks you are about to embark on are going to be a breath of some fresh, much needed air.

As you read through this book that is so beautifully bound in truth, my prayer for you is that God would use it to grow you in relationship with Him, deepen your love for the authority of His holy, infallible Word, and open your eyes to just how beautiful our desperate need for Him truly is.

Soli deo Gloria!

Elle Cardel
Founder of Daughter of Delight (@daughterofdelight)

Daughter of Delight
"A digital women's ministry that supplies
Christ-centered resources, like daily devotionals,
to help women of faith across the globe fully
delight in who He is and the heart He has for His own."

introduction

The phone call from my dad came on a Sunday morning asking if I'd like to join him for brunch. He needed to talk to me about something specific. It was at that brunch in November 2018 that I felt God clearly point out through him that I needed to begin writing again. Though I worried I didn't have the time as a new mom, I knew I couldn't delay my obedience to what God was asking of me. So, as I prayed and wrestled with how to start writing for Him, I prayed about using a podcast platform instead. I felt a covering of peace over me and confirmation that this was a yes from Him after spending time in His Word. Later that week God gave me the words, "Live With Less" which led me to John 3:30, "He must increase but I must decrease." In January 2019, the Living With Less Podcast was born and by God's grace, 1,000's of people have dived deeper into the truths of God's Word. All glory to The King!

Through this journey I continued to feel the Lord put on my heart that one day this would overflow into a devotional that would be in the hands of women, just like me, all over the world. Women who crave a life of less self and more Jesus. Women who desire to live their lives in the freedom of knowing God loves them where they are but loves them too much to leave them unchanged.

My deepest prayer is for this devotional to lead your heart with promptings that challenge, change, and shape your faith. I pray the Lord would do a work in your heart that takes you out of your comfort zone and into the most sacred, deep relationship with Him. Whether you've been walking with the Lord all your life or you have just accepted Christ - this devotional will give your heart a safe place to land, a place to feel seen, and even give you the space to wrestle out the things that get in the way of who Christ calls you to be. You are about to embark on a journey with Him where you will see that the greatest increase in life will be found as you surrender your will to Him. John the Baptist said it best when Jesus began the fulfillment of His earthly ministry. *"He must increase, but I must decrease."*

My favorite part of this project is that you will find an episode from the Living With Less Podcast matched to each week's "More of Him, Less of Me" devotion. This will give you a deeper dive into what you've read, create the space for deeper study in God's Word, and have somewhere to go where it feels like you're in conversation with a trusted friend. I'm so thankful to be on this journey with you and I'm excited to hear all the wonderful ways God works in your life through this devotional!

Lord, I lift up the woman holding this book in her hand. I pray that her heart will be challenged to go deeper with you, changed as she sees what you desire for her life, and shaped as your word permeates every facet of her life. I pray she sees the amazing gift of your grace and mercy poured out over her as she chooses a Christ-centered life in this me-centered world. In Jesus' name, amen.

week one

HE YEARNS FOR US

"For as often as I speak against him,
I do remember him still. Therefore,
my heart yearns for him;
I will surely have mercy on him,
declares the LORD."
Jeremiah 31:20

Have you ever sat wondering, *How can God love the messy parts of me?* As my husband and I journeyed through a hard season in marriage, I sat asking God this question often. We fallen humans are so hard to handle. There is so much about you and me that rebels against Him. Our mouths, our actions (or lack thereof), our attitudes, our addictions, or even the little sins the world deems permissible. By God's grace, the Lord continues to reveal truths from His Word to help give us a deeper sense of clarity on just how much He loves us and why He thinks of us despite our sinful nature.

Look at Jeremiah 31:18-20 with me. It gives a beautiful glimpse of how God thinks of us despite the parts of us that feel very unlovable.

> "I have heard Ephraim grieving, 'You have disciplined me, and I was disciplined, like an untrained calf; bring me back that I may be restored, for you are the LORD my God. For after I had turned away, I relented, and after I was instructed, I struck my thigh; I was ashamed, and I was confounded, because I bore the disgrace of my youth.' Is Ephraim my dear son? Is he my darling child? For as often as I speak against him, I do remember him still. Therefore, my heart yearns for him; I will surely have mercy on him, declares the LORD."

I don't know about you, but this made me weep when I sat with the reality of what this says. Even though our life may be a mess, our marriages might be struggling, or you're living in a season of rebellion, God is yearning for you. Yes, you read that correctly: God is yearning for you. This is hard for us to wrap our minds around, especially as women. It's difficult to think someone can actually love us despite our shortcomings and failures.

Unfortunately, this earthly belief overflows in the way we approach God. We deflect His love by putting earthly conditions on it. We label ourselves unworthy or too disheveled to be loved by Him. We mistake Him for being like one of us.

Ephraim was coming out of a season that I'm all too familiar with, but then God intervened. Scripture shows us many times through stories like Ephraim that our mess doesn't negate His goodness. The Bible is God breathed so all people could see the blueprint for how He calls us to love, live, and lean into the truth of God's Word. Also, for the reminder that God still loves us in the midst of our failures. His heart yearns for us to come running home.

I can just picture the Lord looking me in the eyes as I know I've muttered words similar to Ephraim's and He would whisper back to me, "I remember you still. Therefore, my heart yearns for you; I will surely have mercy on you...".

Next time you find yourself entertaining the lie that God can't handle you and whatever mess you're in because of sin; remember this, God never steps out of His character. He is always loving, good, just, righteous, holy, gracious, truth-filled and in constant pursuit of us. He can't not love you.

Genesis 1:31 says, "And God saw everything that he had made, and behold, it was very good." You and me - made in His perfect image. Made within His hands of perfect, unfailing love. Made for a purpose and plan that He doesn't want to do through anyone else. Let us dig into His Word, tether our hearts to His truths, repent as Ephraim did, and run back to the Lord whose heart is yearning for us.

Lord, help me remember today and every day that your heart yearns for your children. There has never been a moment in my life that you didn't desire to have a relationship with me. Help me have the desire to live with a heart that is tethered to your Word and the truth that you've always loved me. Lord, thank you for always pursuing me and celebrating me when I came running home to you.
In Jesus' name, amen.

thoughts

THE NOOKS AND CRANNIES

"He was pierced for our transgressions;
He was crushed for our iniquities;
upon Him was the chastisement that brought
us peace, and with His words, we are healed."
Isaiah 53:5

While I sat scrubbing the grout in our shower one morning, I found myself knee-deep in conversation with Jesus. My shower is a lot like how most walk into the exciting things in life, especially the Christian life. The idea of white subway tiles with black grout sounds dreamy. It looks esthetically pleasing to the eye. It feels orderly and together. It looks marvelous in photographs and feels like a snapshot of perfection. What people don't see though is the maintenance required: scrubbing each line vertically and horizontally, having to use a specific brush to get into the nooks and crannies. Then, once you've scrubbed and worked hard, you have to tirelessly wipe away the residue over and over.

The idea of this perfect Christian life sounds lovely, too, but it's a life that will come with a promise of dying to self, sanctification, and a need for much grace. A true life with Christ needs Jesus to scrub all the nooks and crannies from our past and present. It takes getting on our knees and changing our perspective from an earthly one to an eternal one. It's living a life that trusts God is taking care of the unseen things. Being a Christian begins with us realizing we need a Savior: Jesus. And if you've picked up this book by choice or by divine appointment, I can tell you with complete certainty that God wants you to know that He sees all the nooks and crannies of your life. He knew about them before you were born and He said, "She's worth it," You, sweet one holding this book, were worth dying for.

"Or do you not know that your body is a temple of the Holy Spirit within you, whom you have from God? You are not your own, for you were bought with a price. So, glorify God in your body." 1 Corinthians 6:19-20

"He was pierced for our transgressions; He was crushed for our iniquities; upon Him was the chastisement that brought us peace, and with His wounds, we are healed." Isaiah 53:5

This is the picture of the Christian life. Jesus came to die on the cross for you and me. So, when you're fed the lies, you are not worth the freedom God desires for you or if you don't seem to believe it, seek His heart through His Word. Let it refresh you, remind you, and restore your spirit. Your Heavenly Father has wanted a relationship with you forever, and these truths are a constant reminder of just how much you mean to Him.

A relationship with the Lord is incredible and challenging all in the same breath. We're promised trials of all sorts; however, within that, we're also promised we will never walk alone for a single moment of it. The conviction, sanctification, seeking, and finding will change your life in ways you could never imagine. He wants to grow a faith in you that is willing and ready to move when He calls. He wants to see your heart tethered to what He says. He wants your life to be centered on Him and what He desires for you. He wants to build up in you a boldness to share about the "Christian life" that you get to live because of Jesus going to the cross.

This week, invite Jesus into the nooks and crannies of your life. Lean into the stirrings of the Holy Spirit as He prompts you to remove what's gotten in the way of Him. Pray for the refreshment of His peace over your heart. Take time this week to journal about what you sense the Lord moving in your heart to remove.

Heavenly Father, help me remember the nooks and crannies of my life
have been some places you've birthed remarkable growth in me.
When my heart becomes weary, remind me even though life will be
laced with trials, there are also stunning victories - and you
see me through ALL of them. In Jesus' name, amen.

thoughts

THE ENEMY WILL STRIKE

"Be sober-minded; be watchful.
Your adversary, the devil, prowls around
like a roaring lion seeking someone to devour."
1 Peter 5:8

The enemy will strike. This is not a cozy statement, but it's the truth, and we need to be ready. The battle will come, and the hard season will hit; if he doesn't come swinging at you, then he will swing at someone you love. Isn't it interesting, too, that some seasons in our life seem almost rhythmic? It's like we know the enemy will sweep in at a certain point because his tactics have been the same time and time again. Still, the seasons lie ahead for all of us where the attack will be a blind-siding disruption to what we felt was stable and good.

Being watchful doesn't mean being fearful, and I think we can blur that line if we're not careful. I remember attending a Bible study where we were studying the Armor of God. As I settled in at my table and the discussion began, I quickly realized that most of the women I was sitting with didn't want to think about the enemy. They lived as if they didn't need to acknowledge him. This showed me the difference between those who are on guard for attacks and those who are fearful of attacks. While I sat there, surprised by these women's reactions to the truth about Satan and what He wants to do to us, I saw first-hand the war being waged against us.

I didn't make it a point to sit at that table again, not because I didn't think they had the wisdom to offer, but I knew I needed older women who could pour into me about how they prepared for, fought, and won the battles. Their responses were all the same: Jesus. These women taught me that when we fight, we do so through obedience. That obedience can look like trusting Him, moving where He's calling you, sitting with Him for extended periods, and trusting He will fight on our behalf. But we, too, have to do the things it takes to stand firm in our faith. (1 Peter 5:9)

We can't learn to be firm in our faith without the trials and attacks that come against us. While I certainly don't want to invite attacks into my life or to those I love, I know it will come. But I also know that God uses everything to teach me more about Him and His character. Let God's will be done.

I don't know the battles you've been up against or the attacks you're watching your loved ones walk through, but I see the faithfulness of the God we serve. We serve the One who defeated the grave. We serve the One who loves you and me so much that He gave us His Word to aid us in being "watchful." The God we serve is the One who stands in the fire with us. He goes before us, He prepares us, He leads us, and He sent His Son Jesus to give us true victory over the enemy.

I want to leave you with this as we head into the week: if our God is for us, then who can stand against us? Who and what do you need to be praying protection over? If this isn't a standard part of your prayer life, then begin this week by claiming the truth from Isaiah 54:17, "No weapon formed against you shall prevail." Pray this for yourself, your home, your loved ones, and anyone God places on your heart.

Lord, I know the enemy is on the hunt to steal, kill, and destroy. As I live my life on the front line for you, Father God, I pray for a faith that can stand firm in moments of attacks. I ask for a mind that quickly remembers your Word and uses it as the powerful weapon it has been promised to stand up against Satan and his demons. I declare I will fight my battles the way you've called us, holding fast, standing firm, and trusting in you.
In Jesus' name, amen.

thoughts

week four

HE IS MOVING

"And those who know your name put
their trust in you, for you, O Lord, have
not forsaken those who seek you."
Psalm 9:10

This title may have made you want to turn the page, skip the week, read ahead. I understand that. Sometimes having someone assure you God is moving can feel like a blanket cultural Christian statement that covers up the fact they have nothing to say. But today, I want you to lean in with me and look at these promises in His Word.

"So, she called the name of the Lord who spoke to her, "You are a God of seeing," for she said, 'Truly here I have seen him who looks after me.'" Genesis 16:13

"And those who know your name put their trust in you, for you, O Lord, have not forsaken those who seek you." Psalm 9:10

"My frame was not hidden from you when I was being made in secret, intricately woven in the depths of the earth." Psalm 139:15

God sees you; He's watching your every move; He's rejoicing over your life—because He created you. He wants you to trust His heart. He wants you to trust that He is moving in all areas of your life, even the ones that look like dead-end roads or a deep desire that hasn't come to pass.

I promise you this: He is moving right now in this moment of your life. It might look different than you hoped. It will probably be more difficult and maybe even a little messy. I don't know what your season looks like, but I know He wants you to lean in closer and have your eyes drift to Him instead of what you hope lies ahead. He wants us to run to His Word before we run to the mouths of others to make His timing make sense or to make the ache of the wait pass.

Honestly, I think a lot of life makes little sense to us with our very limited perspective. Right? Even the best parts of life can leave us scratching our heads and saying, "Did God really do just do that?" I want you to know this. I'm sitting on the bench with you, praying you can trust He is moving in your life even when you can't see it. Someday, you're going to have someone who needs you to whisper these very words to them too because we'll all find ourselves here wondering, "What's God doing, and when will I see Him moving?"

I think Ruth is an excellent example for all of us. She never wavered in her choice to trust what God was doing. It's not that she didn't have hard days (because when we read her story, we see she did). Ruth didn't know what was ahead of her in many circumstances, but she knew who was in charge of her days.

This week as you spend time with the Lord in prayer and in His Word, write the ways you see Him moving, the scriptures He leads you to, and the places in your life that you need to trust Him more. Remember this: when you can't see His hands, always trust His heart.

Heavenly Father, my heart's desire is to know you more and make you known. In this desire, I pray to trust that you are moving even when I cannot see the fruit of the situation I am in. God, thank you for always meeting me within my weakness and showing me your mighty strength. I love you. In Jesus' name, amen.

thoughts

IT TAKES A VILLAGE

"Go into all the world and preach
the good news to everyone."
Mark 16:15

Years ago, I showed up to my very first Bible study. I didn't know a single person in the room. I had no church community, but what I had was a heart hoping for guidance and connection over the Word. I took that uncomfortable step of obedience, and God blessed me by placing my seeking heart under the teaching of a godly woman who deeply desired to grow young women like me in the Word. For the first time in my life, I not only began learning what God's Word said for myself, but I learned what true discipleship looked like. I understood why I needed a village of women to walk alongside me.

As I sit and pen these words, I've just come out of a season that reminds me again why we all need our village—why we need the body of Christ. In this generation, we love the thought of having a village. It sounds incredible to have women encouraging and equipping us with God's truths. But our filled-to-the-brim schedules don't leave any space for this type of discipleship to happen, and the thought of being vulnerable can be paralyzing. Our flesh desires what makes us comfortable, but God calls us to more than comfort.

The Lord tells us,
"Go into all the world and preach the good news to everyone." Mark 16:15

That is not a calling to comfort, but God calls us to move within in the framework in which He places us. So how can we do this if we let fear drive our choice to never change? How will we become part of someone's village if we don't begin taking God's call as a command and not as a suggestion? We act. We act on what His Word tells us to do and then we go. We stay in step with His spirit (Galatians 5:25), press on against the enemies' tactics to control us, and we surrender the insecurities inside of us that keep us in a complacent, cozy faith.

Titus 2 is a place in scripture filled with God's call for women. It calls us to a duty that is high and holy: godly relationships. The Lord asks us to spiritually pour into women who are seeking guidance. We have something unique and special. Our testimonies, which are filled with all the glorious and mundane things God has taken us through. We must not let that inner critic or the enemy trip us up with the lie that we're unequipped. We are equipped in Christ, and when our hearts are tethered to Jesus, we can trust His leading. Women are hungry for truth, but sometimes they might not know where to find it. If you're in their community, you now have the gift of stewarding them to His heart.

> "Older women likewise are to be reverent in behavior,
> not slanderers or slaves to much wine. They are to teach what is
> good, and so train the young women to love their husbands and children,
> to be self-controlled, pure, working at home, kind, and submissive to their
> own husbands, that the Word of God may not be reviled." Titus 2:3-5

I want to leave us pondering a woman from the Bible and her example of following the call to a deeper relationship with others. Ruth showed us what it means to keep showing up for women we care about or the ones God calls us to serve. Ruth left the comfortable to please God. Doesn't this give your heart such encouragement? When God moves you to ask the new woman on your street to coffee or to attend her first Bible study, He isn't surprised by the apprehension of your heart. He knows the call is uncomfortable- He knows it goes against everything in our flesh that clings to familiarity. But He's inviting you and me into something far greater than we can imagine. He's inviting us into being and experiencing His hands and feet. He's trusting us to love, lead, and steward others to Him, and be stewarded by mature believers.

We've got to count the cost of this. If we continue to let fear keep us from extending or accepting invitations to or from other women, we will miss the good things God wants to do in our hearts. Ruth counted the cost. She moved Godward to the community God called her, and I pray my heart can be like hers, don't you? Leaning in, listening, and going when God says, "go."

My prayer for you is that your heart will see the gift God's given you, your story for His glory. I pray we can break free from the fleshly desire of familiarity and that we will move when God calls us. I pray God leads you to women who need to hear the wisdom you offer and trust that God will bring women to come alongside you.

This week ask the Lord to lay on your heart someone who needs to be served by His hands and feet. As He stirs this person or people in your heart, ask Him to lead you in His confidence as you step out in faith to serve them.

Lord, help my heart see the gift God's given me, my story for His glory.
I pray I can break free from the fleshly desire of familiarity. Lord, I pray for
the desire to move when God calls me. Lead me to women who need to
hear about you, and I trust you, Lord, that you will bring women to come
alongside me. In Jesus' name, amen.

thoughts

DIVING DEEPER Living With Less
podcast *Episode 19*

35

week six

RISE UP AND BUILD

"And I told them of the hand of my God that had
been upon me for good and of the words that the
king had spoken to me. And they said, 'Let us rise
up and build.' So, they strengthened their
hands for the good work."
Nehemiah 2:18

Rise and build. These two words can sound empowering and excitingly enticing for a culture that is all about oneself. Our current culture can cause us to pause in embarrassment, even though, at some point, we've all taken the bait. Everywhere we go, we get a dose of the fallen world, and for most of us, we don't even have to walk out the door to experience it. We want to serve ourselves. It's this constant tug between honoring God or honoring ourselves. We can get caught up in this place of thinking, *I'll rise up to the occasion when I feel like it, or when I have more time, or I'll choose which area of God's Kingdom I'd like to help build.* How interesting is it that sin invades, even the way we want to serve the Lord? Thankfully, when we have hearts tethered to Christ, our hearts are full of conviction - amen, amen, amen. That conviction led me to fall in love with Nehemiah's story. This man trusted God in his circumstance, in his waiting, and then on his God-given assignment. He rose to the call God was building him up for.

The story of Nehemiah paints a beautiful picture of letting God call the shots in our lives and following His plans according to His will. In Nehemiah's life, we can clearly see that the words "rise and build" were spoken over his life as a call from the Lord. They had nothing to do with human success but everything to do with our Almighty One. "Rise" in Hebrew means arise, stand, rise, stand. This calls us to action. We must choose to stand up when God calls us. "Build" stood for rebuild, establish, cause to continue. This is the action that takes place from following what God is doing and will continue to do in and through those who do work to expand His Kingdom. This gave my heart such a hope that God not only calls me to action, but He is the one building me up until that process comes to fruition.

As I continued reading Nehemiah's story, I loved seeing when these words in Nehemiah 2:18 were spoken between him and the other men.

"And I told them of the hand of my God that had been upon me for good and of the words that the king had spoken to me. And they said, 'Let us rise up and build.' So, they strengthened their hands for the good work."

It was their mission to do the work of God. Nothing would stop them: no fear from man, no scheme from the enemy. We must ask ourselves: Am I learning His truth as much as I should? Am I leaning into the Holy Spirit the way I'm called? Am I truly on a mission for Christ and His Kingdom, or am I on a mission for what keeps me comfortable? When we wrestle with these things, I think we'll see revival in our hearts take place like these men in His Kingdom, or am I on a mission for what keeps me comfortable? When we wrestle with these things, I think we'll see revival in our hearts take place like these men in Jerusalem. These men fought for the things God was doing where they were. His mission was serious, but they didn't negate the mission because it was a call to build a wall. This is where we must act and rise to where God is calling us. The thing He's calling you to might not look glamorous; maybe it's not something you think you'll enjoy, or perhaps it's loving a person who you think is better off being loved by someone else. This thing He's calling you to might be the very thing that begins rebuilding a heart for Christ.

As this week unfolds, what is God stirring in your heart? What do you keep coming back to that feels more from the spirit than from your own desires? Like Nehemiah, whose heart grieved for what was taking place, he began praying to the Lord about how he could help. In his story, we can see that what his heart began breaking for was the same thing God had planned to use him for in his life. We see this all throughout the Bible. As hearts lean into God and have a deep relationship with Him, their desires line up with what God wants to use them for. So, as we wrestle, pray, ask, and lean in, may we listen for His whisper and hold fast to this truth: "He who has begun a good work in us will bring it to completion" (Philippians 1:6).

Let's pray. Lord, whatever you are building up in us, I pray we will rise to action to move where you're calling. May you remind us that you are the source of our strength, your plans are not like ours, and your heart's mission is to make you known. I ask that you bless us with the courage of Christ to build the Kingdom where you're asking us to be. Let no fear hold us back from the love you want to use to change us and those around us. In Jesus' name, amen.

thoughts

THE CALL OF FORGIVENESS

"For if you forgive others their trespasses,
your Heavenly Father will also forgive you, but if you
do not forgive others their trespasses neither will
your Father forgive your trespasses."
Matthew 6:14-15

Recently, I found myself in a wrestling match with God. I was caught between forgiving or clinging to a hurt He's been asking me to release. It had been stirring for a while, and was clear I needed to move on. I'm sure you've been in this place of wanting God's best but knowing that to begin living in His best, you've got to start by laying down what isn't yours to carry. For months this hurt wreaked havoc over my life. It took the joy out of things I know the Lord was using to bless me, it caused issues in my marriage, and caused me to stumble in my thoughts more times than I'd like to admit. This is what a lack of forgiveness does. It puts the worst of who we are on display for everyone to see and feel.

Jesus talks a lot about forgiveness in the gospels. Reading the words spoken by Jesus holds a weight in my heart that I find nowhere else. When I began processing through the importance of forgiving others who have hurt me, I had to ask, "Why does Jesus talk so much about forgiveness?" The first reason I believe is the very reason Jesus came in the flesh: God sent His one and only Son to pay the price of our sins so we could have a relationship with Him. That is the ultimate act of sacrifice: the gift of forgiveness. I believe He speaks of it so much because we weren't created to carry hurt. God made us in His image, and he never wanted wounds to be a part of our stories.

Matthew 6:14-15 addresses that we must forgive others if we want to be forgiven. For me, when praying this through, I sense God reminding me to trust Him with the judgment and the outcome. Clinging to unforgiveness doesn't create a "judgment" for that person's wrongdoing; however, it establishes corruption in my heart and places me in a false state of authority. Jesus not only came for you and me, but He also came for those who hurt us.

"For if you forgive others their trespasses, your heavenly Father will also forgive you, but if you do not forgive others their trespasses, neither will your Father forgive your trespasses." Matthew 6:14-15

Once we begin to see forgiveness as a gift from God and not a word tossed around with weightless meaning, I believe our hearts will change. We'll see a shift in our lives because we won't be carrying the weight of things in this world that were never intended for us. He wants us to cease carrying what Jesus died for.

Something the Holy Spirit pointed out to me is that the Lord's prayer comes right before this passage in scripture. Matthew 6:12 states a very similar message as verses 14-15 and gives the why behind the need to extend forgiveness. Think about that with me. Jesus, who gave us The Lord's Prayer, included the words, "forgive us our debts, as we have also forgiven our debtors." He said, "as we," not just Him, or you, or me, but we. Therefore, all of us need to experience this and extend it. We can't bypass forgiveness. It's the very essence of who He is, and if He created us to be image-bearers, then it's time to start walking this out as a call and not a suggestion. Let's begin with the small thing, as in the things God has already brought to the surface. Then through processing, forgiving, and loving the way He has called us, we can begin to chisel away at the big things. The things stuffed deep down inside. The things that we can hardly imagine forgiveness scratching the surface of. He wants this freedom for our hearts. Whom the Son sets free, he is free indeed.

Where does your heart need set free? Is there unforgiveness unknowingly hardening you? As this week begins, ask the Lord for the courage to dive headfirst into this call over our lives - to live freely in Him, unbound by chains.

THE LORD'S PRAYER
(Matthew 6:9-14)

"Pray then like this: 'Our Father in heaven, hallowed be your name. Your Kingdom come, your will be done, on earth as it is in heaven. Give us this day our daily bread, and forgive us our debts, as we also have forgiven our debtors. And lead us not into temptation, but deliver us from evil. For if you forgive others their trespasses, your heavenly Father will also forgive you.'" In Jesus' name, amen.

thoughts

week eight

SIT WITH ME, THEN SERVE ME

"But seek first the Kingdom of God and his
righteousness, and all these things
will be added to you."
Matthew 6:33

I had just put my son down for naptime, and per the usual, I thought of the many things I'd like to get done in my hour-and-a-half window. On this day's agenda, I had planned to work on a project the Lord had put on my heart. Completely harmless and thoughtfully obedient, right?! As I sat down to begin my work, the Holy Spirit convicted me, "Sit with me, then serve me."

It led me to ask, why is it so hard to sit with the Lord? It's true, that for many of us, it's easier to jump up and serve Him. This reveals the exact tension between Mary and Martha's hearts.

"Now as they went on their way, Jesus entered a village. And a woman named Martha welcomed him into her house. And she had a sister called Mary, who sat at the Lord's feet and listened to his teaching. But Martha was distracted with much serving. And she went up to him and said, 'Lord, do you not care that my sister has left me to serve alone? Tell her then to help me.' But the Lord answered her, 'Martha, Martha, you are anxious and troubled about many things, but one thing is necessary. Mary has chosen the good portion, which will not be taken away from her.'" Luke 10:38-42

This story often reminds me of where I naturally find myself. Go, go, going for God and missing out on opportunities to sit with Him. Do you find yourself wrestling like this too? Caught in the place of wanting to serve on behalf of the Kingdom doing all the things He's placed on our hearts. But we want it at the unnoticeable expense of our time with Him. What we see play out with Mary and Martha perfectly reflects that we can't let our wanting to do for God get in the way of wanting to be with God.

45

So why is this time so important? Why is it just as important to sit with the Lord and not just serve Him? Two things that come to mind. We can't serve from a desolate, dried-up heart. And we can't be led by the Lord if we don't seek Him for wisdom and understanding. Our time with God is how we grow in our relationship with Him. We learn His Word, we seek His heart, and we take our praises and prayers before Him. So much happens in the moments of quiet, and it's sitting with God that prepares our hearts to serve the Kingdom.

How do we start practically living this out? We look to Jesus and His example. Luke 5:16 tells us that He would draw to desolate places to pray. He, not they. Even Jesus spent time alone with His Heavenly Father. Jesus, the Savior of the world, the sinless Son of God, made it a priority to sit with His Father before serving man. How much more important should this be to us? We need a heart willing to retreat, pray, listen, and then serve.

We need to actively submerge ourselves in His Word, stop overcomplicating worship, and make this time a priority. Your time with Him may look like reading scripture in the carpool line, listening to a solid Christian podcast during rush hour traffic, perhaps it's listening to an audio Bible while you're exercising, or maybe it's sitting in a cozy chair in a quiet house. It doesn't matter where it happens; all that matters is that it does happen.

My prayer for you and me is that we'll find ourselves desiring to lean into the Spirit as it prompts us. I hope you desire to spend time with the Lord and not find yourself constantly seeking to do something for Him. We must stand firm in the truth that when we have hearts filled with the truth, knowledge, and love of Christ, we are then most able to serve the Kingdom from a heart prepared to be the hands and feet of Jesus.

Lord, all you ask of me is to know you and make you known. I can't do either of these if I'm stuck in the pattern of only serving you and not actually knowing you. If this is me currently, please open my eyes to see it. Lord, help me understand that the best place I can find myself is at your feet, learning about you and leaning into the truths of who you are. A heart that deeply knows Christ is a heart that will serve from a place of abundance, and I want to be that woman. In Jesus' name, amen.

46

thoughts

FIGHTING FALSEHOOD

"If you were of the world, the world would love you as its own;
but because you are not of the world, but I chose you out of
the world, therefore the world hates you."
John 15:19

What's happening in the world isn't surprising. The Bible makes it very clear that none of this should catch us off guard. But, when falsehood lands in the pulpit or bible study of your church and community, that changes everything. Suddenly, we see what we've read standing right before our eyes. This unfolded at our former church. While this was heartbreaking, we saw firsthand what happens when the darkness can no longer be contained by those teaching falsehoods.

Through this, I came face-to-face with the truth that those of us sealed by the Spirit will be able to spot the false messages. We will see them for what they are, detriments for the hearts of those who hear them, and abominations to the Lord. These crafty messages laced with the perversion of truth do nothing but tickle itching ears, entice the unsteady souls, and lead people farther from the Lord. And like me, you may find yourself sitting in a church with teachers doing just this, sharing messages that "sound good" but are not in line with the character and Word of God.

So this raises the question we all need to be asking if we come face to face with this situation: what should you do as a believer who upholds the sacred teachings of God's Word? This question may seem extreme but, when you and I claim Christ as Lord and Savior, we don't get to choose which part of God's Word we'll defend. We must honor all of it. We no longer have the option to be hesitant, fearful, and passive Christians as we listen to teachings that are out of alignment with God's word and slithering with enticement to feed off of emotions. We have one option, we must stand up for the truth, and stand firmly against these messages of destruction.

Sisters here is some encouragement. Hold fast and take comfort in what Jesus promised us in John 15:19, "If you were of the world, the world would love you as its own; but because you are not of the world, but I chose you out of the world, therefore the world hates you."

This is what it all boils down to, the world will hate the truth we live by because they first hated Christ, and Christ is truth. Once believers understand that we can no longer seek to please a world that hates our Creator, the true message of the gospel will flourish in a culture that continually shows its depravity.

It's time to take a serious look at who we are allowing to speak "truth" into our lives. Instead of attending the most popular church in your area, look at their values first. Are they Bible teaching or seeker-friendly? Instead of grabbing the newest and most popular Bible studies, take an inventory of who the author is, what they believe, and how they steward their life. Is it one of fame and seeking the glory? Are they swelling with pride as they seek to feed off your feelings? These two things matter much and much more than most Christians think. Friend, take all things before the Lord, hold all things up to scripture, and honor God above all.

Lord, thank you for the gift of your unchanging truth. I pray for boldness and that I always follow your Holy Spirit as my guide. Lead me in conversations to bring your truth to the forefront. Father, if there are destructive teachings in my life, please bring them to the light and expose them for what they are—things that are not of you.
In Jesus' name, amen.

thoughts

THE TRUTH IS WHAT SETS US FREE

"Know the truth, the truth
will set you free."
John 8:32

As I walked through one of my favorite clothing stores, I saw a hutch filled to the brim with beautiful books. Books that I've celebrated as they hit the shelves, and books I found to be earth-shatteringly off about who God is. I felt my heart rate pick up as my skin got hot, and yes, I did what some of you are thinking. I moved the misleading books to the back of the hutch, and I prayed God would keep them hidden. You see, the messages on those pages are being used to mislead and confuse people about who God is to fit their godless agendas. This, my friends, is why God's Word instructs us in 1 Peter 5:8 to be watchful and aware of what the enemy of this world seeks to do.

"Be sober-minded; be watchful. Your adversary, the devil, prowls around like a roaring lion, seeking someone to devour."

We are commanded to be on guard and to stand alert. We must go to the Lord for wisdom and understanding as we grow in discernment. Friend, we're finding ourselves at a pivotal point in history where people seem to be deceived more than ever. The false forms of Christianity have begun to paint a picture that it's easier to build a "life for Christ" around who someone else claims God is, how they interpret what He said, and how His Word should be applied to our lives.

In the same way, we've allowed the size of one's platform to deem them as "truth-tellers," no matter what they say. Many of the ring-leading authors and speakers with the booming platforms are the ones that have created "The feel-good faith." A "faith" that deems sin permissible, elevates false ideologies, and teaches the radical message that faith is about what God can do for you.

I want to tell you something; I write this with tears in my eyes and deep heaviness in my heart. Here is the absolute truth that these messages won't tell

53

you about the Lord. God calls us to take up our cross, die to ourselves, and bear witness to the world. The call over our life is not comfortable or easy. It isn't based on what God can do for us but on what God did and does for His children despite all we did and would do against Him.

> "Then Jesus told his disciples, 'If anyone would come after me, let him deny himself and take up his cross and follow me. For whoever would save his life will lose it, but whoever loses his life for my sake will find it. For what will it profit a man if he gains the whole world and forfeits his soul? Or what shall a man give in return for his soul.'"
> Matthew 16:24-26

As we grow in our knowledge of the heart of God and what His Word says, we will grow in our awareness of the world around us. Through discernment, we'll spot the deception and call it what it is, false teaching. Then by the work of the Holy Spirit and its leading, we in Christ will be able to steward others away from the lies of this world and point them towards a relationship with our Creator.

If you're walking with the Lord, know this: we'll always be living within spiritual tension in this world. We see this reminder all throughout scripture. So as we continue to live in the tensions of this world and point our brothers and sisters to Christ, let us always be quenching our thirst from the purest form of truth, God's infallible Word and our own personal relationship with Him.

This week let us be bold in the confidence we have in Christ. Let us ask the Lord for opportunities to share His truth with those around us. And may we be willing to stand on the front-lines for the Kingdom of God. Pointing people to His Word and away from the false messages of this world.

Lord, help me to remember your truth when the world feels loud. Give me ears that intently listen for your quiet whisper. I pray that my faith would continue to grow as I begin to remove the clutter that has gotten in the way of you. Help me turn to you to quench my spiritual thirst and not the things of this world. Challenge me, change me, and shape me, Lord. In Jesus' name, amen.

thoughts

week eleven

PRIDE GOES BEFORE THE FALL

"For if we live by the spirit, let us
stay in step with the Spirit."
Galatians 5:25

Pride is such a small yet highly destructive word when it's in action. In my life, it seems to start off completely unnoticeable, maybe a random fleeting thought or two. The next thing I know, my pride begins subtracting my ability to acknowledge what God has done and is doing. I seem to shift into a gear of living from an earthly strength rather than leaning on the Lord's strength. Proverbs 16:18 is a concrete reminder of what takes place when pride has stormed through the gates of our hearts.

"Pride goes before destruction and a haughty spirit before a fall."
Proverbs 16:18

This fall includes making a choice to take our eyes off the one we serve and put our eyes on what we want in the flesh. It turns our once innocent and sometimes godly desires into a false way of thinking that everything rests on our abilities. This destruction of pride begins to confuse and manipulate what the will of God looks like to us.

When pride seems to be seeping in the doors of my heart, I often find the Holy Spirit stirring up conviction with Galatians 5:25, "If we live by the spirit, we must stay in step with the Spirit." Because a spirit in step with His leading doesn't want to flirt with the blurry lines that pride places in our midst. A woman truly living out Galatians 5:25 is secure in where God has her and what He wants for her. She trusts what God is doing because she is walking with a heart fully surrendered to Him.

As we grow in our desires to live a life with Christ at the center, and joyfully lay down our pride, our heart becomes the fertile ground for submission to the Lord, and sanctification. This is a guard against destruction.

It's easy to spot someone who has a heart on fire for Christ and fully trusts what God is doing. Galatians 5:25 seeps out of them. They look drastically different than those living their life hinged on pride and placing their hope on their abilities.

At the end of the day, we're not here for ourselves and our glory, and it takes a humble heart to willfully accept that. My prayer for all of us this week is that we would live our lives according to God's will, His ways, and rest in the truth that He desires humble hearts that want to glorify Him.

Take some time in prayer this week and journal about the desires you have in your heart. Hold them up to scripture to see if they are rooted in pride or in alignment with the leading of the Spirit.

Lord, we stand in the truth that you are for us, and we are so thankful that your heart rejoices in the people who love you. God, I pray that any ounce of pride or sinful desire taking our eyes off you would be revealed and removed from our lives. Lord, we ask that you fill the place in our hearts that have been filled with the things that are not of you.
In Jesus' name, amen.

thoughts

OPEN HANDS, OPEN HEART

"Trust in the Lord with all your heart,
and do not lean on your own understanding."
Proverbs 3:5

What does open-handedly trusting God look like for you? For me, it means letting go of the very things I want to control. I want complete control over my marriage, I grapple with wanting to have full say in every choice our children will ever make, and I want to know that my health will sustain me for many years. You, too, have possibly wanted to have control over these very things. But the truth is, you and I know this desire for control doesn't line up with what God's Word asks of us. He tells us this...

"Be wise not in your own eyes; fear the Lord, and turn away from evil."
Proverbs 3:7

"I have chosen the way of faithfulness; I set your rules before me. I cling to your testimonies, O Lord; let me not be put to shame! I will run in the way of your commandments when you enlarge my heart."
Psalm 119:30-32

We're called to turn away from what takes our eyes off the Lord, and we're also reminded that we can't control anything but our obedience to Him. We won't find wisdom from our flesh, true wisdom is only found in Christ. This too, goes for wanting complete control. It stems from the sinful desires of the flesh, causing us to think we're wiser than the One who created us.

Proverbs 3:5 pierced my heart one evening as I sat trying to understand why I had been feeling so much angst. His Word revealed to me that I will not experience the wisdom and refreshment of the Lord if I'm constantly giving myself over to the desire for full control. This is true for you, too.

After this conviction set it, the Lord began an open-heart surgery on me and showed me what it meant to live open-handedly for Him. He made me trust Him with my husband, which turned into deeper intimacy with prayer. He took my worries about our children's choices and turned them into reminders that they are God's children first, and He loves them more than I could ever imagine. He's used several unexplained health issues to teach me that He will sustain me through whatever I face. Through this conviction, God showed me that my desire to control is not only an area of sin, but something only He can remove and restore.

This led me to look at Joseph's story from Genesis 37 and what a life story he has. Joseph had to fully trust where God had him in circumstances he didn't desire for himself. He was hated by his brothers, who sold him into slavery. He was thrown into prison for adulterous accusations, yet Joseph continued to trust the Lord. While he trusted God, God continued to orchestrate incredible things in and through his life. We can learn a lot from Joseph's story. We can see that our seasons where we lack control are often the ones that push us to a deeper relationship with the Lord. It causes us to trust God's heart and to find refuge and refreshment in His Word.

Where are you today? Are you in the middle of a spiritual open-heart surgery? Have you just started the healing process from the procedure? Or are you seeing that it's time for you to invite God into those hard places? Wherever you find yourself today, I pray that you see the deep need for trusting in Him. I pray that you know a life of living open-handed for Christ will be the most freeing thing you will experience and the most sanctifying. Ask the Lord to show you where you are spiritually and to lead you as you take an inventory of your heart. Write down the areas of your life you struggle with when it comes to releasing control.

Lord, as you reveal the things in my heart that need tending, help me fully surrender them to you. Help me see, like Joseph, that you are always working things out for good, even when I don't see them. God, I pray that my heart will always desire to trust you and not lean on my own understanding. In Jesus' name, amen.

thoughts

week thirteen
LORD OF ALL

"I am the vine; you are the branches.
Whoever abides in me and I in him,
he it is that bears much fruit, for apart
from me, you can do nothing."
John 15:5

I'll never forget the fall that the Lord did some intense pruning in my life. It was a particularly beautiful one that seemed to fit the exact season I was in. Branches being pruned so that once again, new life could be brought forth.

For years I had some really tough questions that swirled around in my heart, but I never knew how to bring them before the Lord. I felt like I was lacking in faith for what I wanted to understand. There was even an inkling of fear that hovered in my heart anytime the questions would arise. Finally, that fall, I realized the anxiety and concern for asking questions weren't coming from the goodness of God's heart but from the one who wanted to keep me from growing deeper in my relationship with the Lord. I'm sure you've been in these seasons, too.

"The thief comes only to steal and kill and destroy.
I came that they may have life and have it abundantly."
John 10:10

The enemy didn't want me taking my questions to the Lord. Why? Because He knows God is faithful to lead us to wisdom and understanding. I decided to press in and no longer let the enemy have this grip on me. I wanted to know more about God's heart and seek His Word for answers to my questions.

Through this season, the Lord began stripping me of the pride, fear, and angst that continued to keep me from having that deeper relationship with Him. He showed me the importance of putting my relationship with Him over everything. As the weeks passed, God had continued to lead me through the Old Testament, somewhere I'd never spent much time.

I learned so much about Him that my years of hesitation and fear kept from me. I saw God's heart from a different perspective and got to see His honor and love for those who keep His Word. I learned so much about our family in Christ and all they walked through out of reverence to Him. I became even more aware that we need to seek to know Him because we can do nothing apart from Him. I saw that we can't do anything well when we haven't surrendered our desires to Him.

The book of Exodus surprisingly became a favorite of mine. Each day I spent time here, I felt the Lord gave me the wisdom, clarity, and discipline to get through it. This taught me why we need to just keep showing up and lean into His sufficiency's. Chapter-by-chapter, I actually saw the similarities between my life and the Israelites. Not so much culturally, but in the character and condition of our hearts.

Did you know a generation of the Israelites missed the Promised Land because they disobeyed God? They allowed fear to override the promise God had spoken to them.

> "The Lord your God who goes before you will himself fight for you, just as he did for you in Egypt before your eyes, and in the wilderness, where you have seen how the Lord your God carried you, as a man carries his Son, all the way that you went until you came to this place. Yet in spite of this word, you did not believe the Lord your God, who went before you in the way to seek you out a place to pitch your tents, in fire by night and in the cloud by day, to show you by what way you should go."
> Deuteronomy 1:30-32

We are still just as fallen as these men and women. God commanded them to "go", and they let their fear of man get in the way. Our disobedience—whether it's delaying, fear, or pride—does the same thing. It comes with a cost, and it comes with consequences.

I want to tell you something. Giving the Lord, Lordship over our lives isn't intended to shackle us—*it's to free us.* We see this theme throughout the Old Testament and New Testament, like when Jesus tells us in John 15:5, "I am the vine; you are the branches. Whoever abides in me and I in him, he it is that bears much fruit, for apart from me you can do nothing."

This week ask the Lord if fear is keeping parts of your heart from Him. Study what it means to have the Lord rule and reign over all and journal what you learn as you begin to process through.

> *Jesus, today I choose you over everything else. I want what you want. I want my life to look like yours. I know this comes with a cost to my life, but it's one well worth it. Help me to live a life of decrease so you may increase. I desire a heart that doesn't skimp out on the "promised land" to feed my fleshly desires. I pray for a faith that chooses obedience immediately and not as an afterthought. Lord, lead me to places in your word that will help me better understand you and the character of your heart.*
> *In Jesus' name, amen.*

thoughts

TRADING AN ANXIOUS LIFE
FOR A HOPE-FILLED FUTURE

"Jesus was in the stern, sleeping on a cushion.
The disciples woke him and said to him,
'Teacher, don't you care if we drown?'"
Mark 4:38

Palms sweating, heart pounding, throat tightening. These three things defined several years of my life. I vividly remember sitting in my car, tears pouring from my eyes, calling my pastor, and saying, "I'm reading God's truth and saying it out loud. Why isn't anything changing?" I was desperate for an answer to heal what I was feeling, but that is not what I got.

Years later, I'm so thankful for that phone call with my pastor because he taught me that in those desperate places, God's word isn't magic; but it's through His living word that He teaches us and leads us through our hard moments and seasons. That day, I learned this: *Jesus is in my boat*, but that doesn't mean He will instantly remove suffering or answer prayers. It means that He promises to be with me and see me through the storm. He wants my thoughts to be focused on Him, instead of me being disillusioned by my circumstance.

Looking back, my long season of anxiety often takes me to the story of the disciples in the boat with Jesus from Mark 4:37-39.

"And a great windstorm arose, and the waves were breaking into the boat, so that the boat was already filling. But he was in the stern, asleep on the cushion. And they woke him and said to him, 'Teacher, do you not care that we are perishing?' And he awoke and rebuked the wind and said to the sea, 'Peace! Be still!' And the wind ceased, and there was a great calm."

While the storm was raging around them, Jesus was sleeping. Why would Jesus keep sleeping amid their fear during a storm in which they felt they would drown? This is a valid question and one that I'm sure we've all found ourselves asking within seasons that looked like we might drown if they lasted any longer. For many years, the moments I felt I was drowning, I'd find myself calling someone who I felt could help keep my head above the water, someone who would listen and validate my feelings. While this approach might have felt good at the moment, I know it's not the approach God desires for us.

When we look at Mark 4:38, we can't miss this detail mentioned, Jesus was "sleeping on a cushion." Jesus was completely comfortable where He was. He was the perfect example of the peace we can have when we call on Him. Jesus did awaken, but it was only when the disciples went to Him. Isn't that amazing? I praise God for this minor detail. It's a reminder of why we need to always pursue Christ. He wants us to acknowledge Him. Jesus wasn't oblivious to the raging storm going on around them. Their anxieties did not catch him off guard because He is all-knowing. He just wants His followers to trust in Him no matter what we're facing, and it's through these experiences that He purifies and sanctifies us. He uses these moments to teach us more about His character, and why we undeniably need Him.

Truthfully, the more I've faced anxiety or anxious thoughts, the more opportunities I've received to invite the Lord in and stand firm in the confirmation He is with me. I cling to the facts that He is all-knowing, He is the Author of each day, He is the Alpha, Omega, Beginning, End, He is just, and He loves me deeply.

Our faith in the Lord will not exempt us from affliction because we live in a fallen world. But what our faith gives us, is confidence in Christ to walk through all the uncomfortable situations we'll face. For me, what started as a season of loneliness and wondering where God was, later became the season He used to bring me to a place of knowing I am seen by our Creator; I am never out of His sight. Remember that Jesus is in your boat when you face events that cause your anxiety to flare or trigger anxious thought patterns.

This week, call on Him when waters feel like they're rising, trust in Him when you start to feel uncertainty clouding your thoughts, and cling to Him as He sees you through your raging storms.

As the storms of life rage around me, Jesus help me to see you as my anchor. I pray for a heart that invites you into my feelings of anxiety and fear. God, I ask that you continue to build in me a faith built on your solid rock. Jesus, I invite you into my boat. I trust you. In Jesus' name, amen.

thoughts

OUR CONFIDENCE IN CHRIST

"I call upon you, for you will answer me, O God;
incline your ear to me; hear my words."
Psalm 17:6

Knowing the promise, we have to call upon the Lord brings my soul a deep sense of peace and humility because it's so undeserved. The security of protection and provision He offers us despite our selfishness is unlike anything we will ever experience on this side of eternity.

My life before Christ certainly wasn't one that felt like it should have this type of lavish love laid upon it. A love that changed me from the inside out by the gift of sanctification.

For someone so reckless in rebellion, stuck in a self-centered way of living, and having eyes set on a worldly standard of life, it felt like an outlandish thought that I would ever experience the grace of God. But, because God sent His Son Jesus to pay the price of my sins, once I received Him in my heart, I too received His grace and His mercy—and I pray you to know that for yourself, too. This is what our confidence is rooted in: the God who sees, saves, and sent His Son to take our place.

We see all throughout scripture that we can call upon the Lord in confidence. We see this often taking place in the Psalms from the heart of King David. David knew full well God would be faithful to answer him, with rebuke and reproof but also with His mercy. I love the confidence we see in Psalm 17.

"My steps have held fast to your paths; my feet have not slipped. I call upon you, for you will answer me, O God; incline your ear to me; hear my words. Wondrously show your steadfast love, O Savior of those who seek refuge from their adversaries at your right hand. Keep me as the apple of your eye; hide me in the shadow of your wings, from the wicked who do me violence, my deadly enemies who surround me." Psalm 17:5-9

David prayerfully calls out, pleading to God in crisis for protection from his enemies. Yes, this is the same David, who was not only called the man after God's own heart but an adulterer and murderer. He fell into sin, experienced consequences but still trusted he could confidently turn to the Lord because he had a deep love and reverence for his relationship with Him.

I can vividly recall seasons in my life where I wish I would've cried out to God, but I believed in my flesh that I could muddle through on my own. My sin felt too heavy to work through, and the shame that filled me kept me from being honest with our Creator. My desire to suppress my sin clouded my confidence in Christ. But I want to remind you something, God doesn't call us to muddle through hard things; He calls us to surrender all things to Him. He calls us to confidently approach His throne of grace (Hebrews 4:16). He wants to guide our hearts through conviction as we experience the gift of His redeeming love over every area in our life.

This is when things begin shifting. As our confidence in Christ expands, we start seeing God for who He is and who we are. He is holy, just, kind, merciful, all-knowing, all-truthful, beginning, and end. We are broken, frail people—created in the image of God but those who desperately need a Savior.

As we confidently call upon the Lord, we will see that He's always pursuing, leading, and loving us. He draws us deeper as we see He longs for us to call out to Him. He desires for us to be humbled by His grace, and to see Him as the only one who can deliver us, renew us, and redeem us.

This week as we live out our faith with hearts boldly and confidently chasing after God, seek His heart and ask the Holy Spirit to stir up the places within you to greater faith in approaching God. Journal what He lays on your heart and pray for His guidance as you unpack what He leads you to. Come back in a few weeks to write more on what you've felt God teaching you. Reflect on what part of His Word you've gained a better understanding of regarding confidence in Christ.

Lord, help me to see you for who you are and not who I want you to be. As I learn more about your attributes and grow in deeper confidence, remind me to call out to you. Help me see that you're always ready to redeem me. Jesus, thank you for pursuing my heart.
In Jesus' name, amen.

thoughts

week sixteen

WHAT ARE YOU SEEKING?

"For where your treasure is, there
your heart will be also."
Matthew 6:21

I can go all the way back to my early teen years and pinpoint exactly what my heart deeply longed for *contentment*. This didn't stop after I exited the walls of high school but continued into adulthood. I spent years seeking to fill the empty void within my heart through every earthly avenue. I believed the lie that contentment would finally settle in through any *new* thing. New ruled and reigned over my life as an idol of false hope and fleeting feelings. Maybe this has been something you've struggled with too?

When the newness of whatever I'd taken refuge in wore off and didn't meet the expectations I hoped it would, I'd sit empty-handed thinking, *Why can't I fix this feeling?* This gaping hole that I wanted to be filled so badly obviously couldn't be filled with a "thing" but needed to be filled with Jesus. I can still do this sometimes, and maybe you do that too. My heart gets wrapped up in thinking that something new will fix what is broken inside me. When the answer is: *only Christ can fix what's broken.*

When we choose "things" to heal brokenness, I believe we only become more broken. Jesus said in Matthew 6:20, "But lay up your treasures in heaven, where neither moth nor rust destroys and where thieves do not break in and steal." This scripture alone reminds us that we cannot seek contentment in the things of this world. Doing so disregards the promise we're given in Christ. Maybe you're wondering what does God promises us when it comes to contentment? Can we really be content in Christ while here on earth?

Yes, you can. Contentment in Christ means having an eternal perspective as we live out our earthly mission for the Kingdom. Our contentment in Him looks like setting our minds on the treasures of heaven and what awaits us. It's living out our convictions and tethering our hearts to God's standard of living. I write this from a place of deep conviction because I can get this so wrong.

Jesus tells us in John 10:14, "I am the good shepherd. I know my own and my own know me." Jesus knows about the gaping holes in our hearts. He isn't surprised when you and I turn to things to fill us, but He most certainly doesn't rejoice in that. When He sees us begin to blur the lines with things that pull us from Him, He knows what suffering will come along with it.

We all should realize in these seasons of seeking contentment elsewhere, our heart never stops longing for what only the Lord can fill. This week I encourage you to turn to the Lord and ask the Holy Spirit to reveal what's ruling you. Is it your possessions, your relationships, or is it, Jesus? Let the power of conviction lead you away from sin and into the life, God desires for you as His beloved child. He creates beauty from ashes and turns mourning into joy. His relationship restores brokenness and gives rest to a weary wandering heart. Look to Him as your treasure.

God, I desire to live a life that seeks you first and foremost. I pray for a discipline that seeks to live my days fully for you, with YOUR agenda in mind, not my own. God, I ask you to reveal to me the things that I've made more valuable than my relationship with you. I ask that you lead me as I learn to place you on the throne of my whole life, not just the parts I'm willing to give up. I love you, Lord. In Jesus' name, amen.

thoughts

WHAT'S YOUR MISSION?

"The one who calls you is faithful,
and He will do it."
1 Thessalonians 5:24

The other week, I sat across the table from a friend. With her heart heavy, she shared, "I don't know what my purpose is. All I do is sit behind a desk and clock forty hours a week." I wanted to affirm her and boost her confidence at that moment, but I realized my words can't heal her aching heart – *only God can.*

As I sat looking back at her, all I could say was this, "God created all of us with purpose; sometimes we just have to look at our life from a different perspective." What I meant by that was this: we don't need a platform, thousands of followers, likes on social media posts, and bursting-at-the-seams in-home Bible studies to prove we're living out God's purpose for our life. We need to live our lives obediently following Christ, and from that posture, His mission for us flows.

1 Thessalonians 5:23-24 tells us, "Now may the God of peace himself sanctify you completely and may your whole Spirit and soul and body be kept blameless at the coming of our Lord Jesus Christ. He who calls you is faithful; he will surely do it."

Do you see the promise and provision God gives us through His Word? He will call us, equip us, and sanctify us through the mission He has handpicked for our lives. Personally, I believe, the most extraordinary mission for the Kingdom begins when the Great Commission pierces our hearts. We see what we are truly living for; *to know Christ and make Him known.*

We get caught up in thinking that to serve God, it has to be big and exciting. When in reality, the God we serve is the one who makes the ordinary everyday things extraordinary moments for the Kingdom. When I think of Jesus and His ministry, I think of how He met so many people in their mundane moments. Jesus didn't only pick the people of utmost importance, but He also didn't choose just the lowly. He met with all people wherever God placed Him.

God does the same thing with us. He equips us where He has us. He asks us to obey His leading and trust Him as we seek to live out the Kingdom mission He has for us. Through this, we get to watch Him peel back the layers in our own lives that challenge, change, and shape us to know Him better and serve His Kingdom the way He desires.

I pray you see the beauty in living out the specific mission God has given you. Trust that whatever He has called you to is what He will use to sanctify you as He draws you closer to His heart. Perhaps the mission God has called you to in this season is right under your nose: to bless who sits next to you at work, to pray for the barista you see daily as you pick up your coffee, or perhaps extend extra help to your neighbor.

He's entrusted a special mission to you and me. One that He sees perfectly as it unfolds from His viewpoint. Know this, you are a part of His mission field, and He will use your obedient heart. This week, love one of those people He constantly has in your midst, ask Him to give you clarity through His Word if you're to be serving somewhere specific. Make a list of all the ways you've previously seen God use you, big or small. Write them out to remind you that God desires to use you whether that is behind a desk or in the heart of your home.

Heavenly Father, as I step out into this day, I pray for eyes that see through your perspective. I pray for a heart that desires your mission and not my own. Help me to see those who need you. Help me see the areas of my life that are getting in the way of who you're calling me to be.
In Jesus' name, amen.

thoughts

LOVING, LEADING, TEACHING, PURSUING

"They said to the woman, 'It is no longer because of what you said that we believe, for we have heard for ourselves, we know that this is indeed the Savior of the world.'"
John 4:42

At some point in our lives, we'll need the reminder that the Lord is always pursuing our hearts. He doesn't just stop pursuing us once we surrender our lives to Him; the pursuit keeps going, and our relationship only grows deeper.

I remember sitting at a Palm Sunday service several years ago where I first heard a teaching on the Woman at the Well. As this woman's story was shared, I'll never forget the peace that covered me. This story showed me that the Lord always wanted me, and I want you to know that He has always wanted you too. His heart has yearned for us when we've been far from Him and even still when we're near to Him. He's loved us the same, and He's never contemplated stopping.

John 4 paints one of the most beautiful pictures in the Bible. It puts into perspective that the things this woman was feeling match the very things you and I have felt in some way, shape, or form. We've all felt shame, guilt, worry, and insecurity. This woman's story with Jesus gives us full assurance of the pursuit we read about all through scripture – from Genesis to Revelation.

For me, a favorite part of her story is when she tells Jesus she "knows the Messiah is coming." Here's a woman whose life has been plagued by sin, yet she knows of the hope in the long-awaited Savior of the world. Then Jesus says to her, "I who speak to you am He."

Can you imagine this moment? The Messiah looking you in the eyes and sharing that it is He. I can only imagine what her heart felt like at that moment: relief, joy, hope, love, and probably utter shock that Jesus chose to reveal himself to her. We know for sure that she felt so confident in what had happened that she ran and told her people all about the Messiah, and many believed.

"Many Samaritans from that town believed in him because of the woman's testimony, 'He told me all that I ever did.' So when the Samaritans came to him, they asked him to stay with them, and he stayed there two days. And many more believed because of his word. They said to the woman, 'It is no longer because of what you said that we believe, for we have heard for ourselves, and we know that this is indeed the Savior of the world.'" John 4:39-42

It's incredible when we think about what the heart of God does. It loves, leads, teaches, and pursues. Because of Jesus pursuing this woman, we can stand firm in this. If He pursued the woman at the well, then He absolutely pursues you. If Jesus took the time to teach this woman about the living water, He desires to teach you about Himself too. Remember that He knows you and wants you to know Him and seek His heart. Through this incredible grace over our lives, we then, just like her, get to share what He has done in our hearts!

When you look at your life story, do you see a moment at the well? Perhaps you see many moments at the well. I look back and see many seasons where I once again needed a refreshing through the promises of God. His arms are always wide open ready to bring restoration to our souls.

This week, take the time to ask the Lord what you need to lay down in your life that's taking your eyes off Him? What part of your life needs tending to so, you can experience the restoration He offers to His children? Journal what comes to mind and write prayers for each specific thing.

Heavenly Father, thank you for the constant reminders that you care for us, love us, lead us, teach us, and pursue us. God, help me see in the seasons of difficulty that the hard work which comes with restoration and redemption is worth it. I pray for a heart that yearns to rest and trust in all you have for me. Thank you for being intentional in your pursuit of me and making me feel loved in the seasons I didn't deserve it. God, may I always turn and run to you. In Jesus' name, amen.

thoughts

week nineteen

THE GOD WHO SEES

"So, she called the name of the Lord who
spoke to her, 'You are a God of seeing,'
for she said, 'Truly here I have seen him
who looks after me.'"
Genesis 16:13

Many of us struggle with feeling seen. This ebb and flow are something I believe we can all relate to. Sadly, too often in the mainstream Christian sphere, we're directed towards being sold the message that we are seen by the authors, speakers, leaders, and so on, all at the expense of hearing that we are seen by our Creator. This is heartbreaking, and it's leaving hearts more broken than mended in Christ. It's created women who would rather seek earthly gratification of being seen by the world rather than understanding that God Almighty sees us.

You see, while it feels good to know those around notice us, there is an indescribable joy we have once we know there's not a moment that God's eyes are off you and me. He sees us in the seasons of devastation, betrayal, heartache, and joy. He sees us in victory, healing, and celebration. He not only shows us that He sees us, but He tells us that He sees us in this Word...

He saw Eve in the garden. (Genesis 3:13)

He saw Hagar in the desert. (Genesis 16:13)

He saw Leah in her heartbreak. (Genesis 29:31)

He saw Rehab's red cord. (Joshua 2:18)

He saw Hannah in her suffering. (1 Samuel 1:11)

He saw Bathsheba in her adultery. (2 Samuel 11:4)

He saw Mary in her obedience. (Luke 1:28)

He saw the Woman at the Well with her weary soul. (John 4:26)

This is the best news; we are seen by God Almighty. The Creator of Heaven and Earth sees you and me. Not only does He see us, but we are pursued by Him daily. By sending His Son to the cross because of His deep love for us, we are sealed by the blood of Jesus.

Our Heavenly Father wants you to look to Him in the seasons when you wonder if anyone notices you because He does. He always has, and He always will. He wants to lead you, love you, and sanctify you wholly. This is why we have to dive into His Word, write it on our hearts, and make our relationship with the Lord of utmost importance. When we do this, we no longer sway to and fro but can hold fast to the promises of God and not the validation of other fallen people.

This week take the time to write these eight scriptures out listed on the previous page. Tape them in the places you'll see them often. This way, you're reminded of the Father we serve and the promise that He sees you.

Heavenly Father, I pray that as I seek to know you more deeply, my desire to be validated by the world diminishes. I pray in my moments of weakness that I will remember the promises you gave us in scripture. Lord, thank you for always pursuing me and desiring to make yourself known to me. In Jesus' name, amen.

thoughts

week twenty
MY GUIDE

"Nevertheless, I am continually with you;
you uphold my right hand.
You guide me with your counsel, and afterward
you will receive me to glory."
Psalm 73:23-24

Frustrated, sad, and worried seemed to describe the state of my heart in a not-so-long-ago season of my life, which quite honestly may still be lingering some days. All the feelings that I had were understandable given the circumstance, but God wasn't asking me to carry the weight of what was unfolding. I layered up and went out for a walk on a crisp Sunday morning. I listened to our Pastor's sermon while I pounded the pavement beneath my feet. As the sermon ended, I felt I needed to spend a long time in worship. If you're like me, then sometimes you can get caught up in hearing about God while simultaneously forgetting to experience Him. I began listening to old worship songs, or hymns as many of us know them. *Holy, Holy, Holy, Lord God Almighty* began playing through my ears and pierced my weary soul. The sadness of my heart seemed to surface as the lyrics played...

"Holy, holy, holy!

Though the darkness hide thee

Though the eye of sinful man

Thy glory may not see

Only Thou art holy

There is none beside Thee

Perfect in power, in love and purity."

Friend, the Lord is love and purity. He is holy. He is truth. He is worthy. He is almighty. My eyes welled with tears as these truths were sung into my ears which overflowed into my heart. This is how we experience Him, not just through a song, but when we lay down our life to fully embrace His heart. We bask in the truth of God's almighty holiness. Within the righteousness of God, we experience the goodness of God, the mercy of God, and the grace of God. God's invitation to us is one laced with much good and much sanctification. This means when we accept the invitation, He will be our guide, counsel, refuge, and safe place. He is the one who lights the lamp to the path we walk and will hold our hands as we walk through seasons of joy and suffering.

God makes it clear all throughout His Word why we need Him, and I needed Him that morning – just like I need Him every day. In Psalm 73:28, it tells us, "but it's good for me to be near God; I have made the Lord my refuge, that I may tell of all your works." When our hearts seek nearness to God, we better understand our deep need for Him. When He is our refuge, we see His heart tangibly permeating all facets of our lives. I want to remind you of this, He's a good Father, the best Father, no matter what our circumstances look like.

I pray our seasons of difficulty are not easily forgotten. I pray these seasons are the ones that leave us more tethered to Christ–more than we were before the difficulty came. I pray you'll join me in taking time this week to better understand who God is and what a gift we have under the almighty authority of His holiness. As you spend time with Him, ask that He quiets your heart as He speaks His truths to your soul through His Word. Journal about a few of the challenging seasons you've walked through and how you saw the Lord leading you every step of the way.

Lord, how faithful you are. Thank you for giving us your Word as an example of what living for you looks like. Help me to live a life that is focused less on myself and what saddens, frustrates, and worries me. Help me to live a life that increases in knowledge of you as my guide as I live to make you known. In Jesus' name, amen.

thoughts

week twenty-one

BUT, EVEN IF NOT

"Before I was afflicted, I went astray,
but now I keep your word.
You are good and do good;
teach me your statutes."
Psalm 119:67-68.

But even if not, He is still good. Chances are, you've seen or heard this phrase in your life. It hangs on the walls at home décor stores, and it's often beautifully written on t-shirts, but it makes me ask myself, is this genuinely written on our hearts? "Do I really believe that God is still good even if hard seasons, unanswered prayers, and tragic happenings become my reality?" This is one of those questions that can keep us up at night. It causes us to wrestle, ask, and seek His clarity.

I still vividly remember the day when depression and anxiety became a cloud looming over me. For months following, I struggled to even get out of bed. I didn't feel like myself anymore, and at this point in my very new walk with the Lord, I didn't understand where God was or what He was doing. I'd awake in the wee hours of the morning to grab my devotional, hoping that something would make the anxiety and depression disappear. I remember wondering in this season of despair, *Is He really good?*

Yes. He is still good—He always has been and always will be. Not because the season of affliction lifted but because God is always sovereign; He permits, wills, and leads us through everything we face. Personally, what I didn't see until about a year-and-a-half after this depression and anxiety set in was that God used this season of anxiety and depression to land me into the chair of a Christian counselor, to get out of a non-God honoring relationship. Best of all, He led me to my husband and the church that helped to flourish my love for the Lord and His Word. As I look back on the season of prayers and wrestling with the "if not's," I see the whole time I was facing affliction, God was there sustaining me each day.

Through that season, Psalm 119 became a favorite passage of mine. Prayerfully read this portion of scripture and ask the Lord to open your eyes to the sharpening that flows from affliction:

"You have dealt well with your servant, O Lord, according to your word. Teach me good judgment and knowledge, for I believe in your commandments. Before I was afflicted, I went astray, but now I keep your word. You are good and do good; teach me your statutes. The insolent smear me with lies, but with my whole heart, I keep your precepts; their heart is unfeeling like fat, but I delight in your law. It is good for me I was afflicted that I might learn your statutes. The law of your mouth is better to me than thousands of gold and silver pieces." vs.65-72

The Lord used this season to teach me why I needed to know His Word and write it on my heart. He used this to show me why I needed a hunger and thirst for much more than a short daily devotion; I needed to look to Him as my sustainer.

As you and I walk through our life with Christ, we will be faced with moments and seasons that make us ask the hard questions. Our journeys with the Lord will not always be pretty. This is a journey of sanctification and humility, which equates to hard days for us in the flesh. But while we endure this, we can have full assurance that we will learn much about the heart of God, and it will always be worth it.

Are you walking through the fires of affliction, or do you know someone who is? Do you or someone you know need the reminder that God is still good? I want to share this scripture with you, and I pray you share it with the ones who need this reminder to...

"My sheep hear my voice, and I know them, and they follow me. I give them eternal life, and they will never perish, and no one will snatch them out of my hand. My Father, who has given them to me, is greater than all, and no one is able to snatch them out of the Father's hand. I and the Father are one." John 10:27-30.

God, you are good, no matter what my circumstances say. Help me see this on the days I'm struggling. Help me rest in the full assurance that you're always working things out in the unseen. Lord, as I walk through affliction, remind me you are there. In Jesus' name, amen.

thoughts

TRUSTING GOD DURING GRIEF

"The king was overjoyed and gave orders to
lift Daniel out of the den. And when
Daniel was lifted from the den, no wound
was found on him because
he had trusted in his God."
Daniel 6:23

I can still see the Sunday morning sun piercing through the windows as I got dressed to meet my friend for our pre-church coffee date. In this season, my husband and I were prayerfully trying to become pregnant. That morning, as I bent over to grab my jeans from the drawer, I felt the Lord gently stir in my heart that my friend was pregnant. My heart sank, and grief washed over me.

I cried out to the Lord, "Why not me!?" "Why can't I be content with where you have me?" This was a pivotal point in my walk with Jesus. I quickly realized joy can't be based on my circumstances or hinge on prayers answered in the way I desire.

This brings me to Daniel in the lion's den, which gets lots of attention from Christians, and it should. It's an absolute miracle by the Lord! What often comes to mind for me, though, is Daniel's supernatural peace and joy in Christ through all that led up to that moment.

Daniel's life story shows us the importance of having a heart that trusts what God is doing, even when we cannot trace His hands. Daniel's trust in God wasn't based on his earthly circumstance. Daniel knew the Lord would lead Him, sustain Him, and work everything out for His great purpose.

Because we live in a fallen world, we will undoubtedly find ourselves in places of pain and gut-wrenching grief. These seasons will always find their way onto the pages of our story. While God never desired for suffering to plague our lives, sin brought it forth, but it's by God's grace and mercy that He's given us a way to be delivered from it all. The gift of Jesus, the gift of our salvation, and the gift of the Holy Spirit dwelling in you and me.

As we end our time looking at Daniel's life, I want to focus on his example to pray without ceasing. In this story, even though a law was put into place stating he could not pray to His Father, Daniel abided in the heart of God. He never stopped pursuing the heart of God. This applies to all of us too. We can never stop seeking God no matter what our life circumstance looks like.

Don't let the grief, uncertainty, or waiting that you're experiencing steal the trust you have in the heart of your Heavenly Father. Your life is a testimony being written by the Lord, and He is using this season for a purpose. Daniel's testimony of God's protection not only was for a work in Daniel's heart, but God also used it in the heart of King Darius. (Daniel 6:1-28)

I am thankful that God didn't leave this season of grief and waiting out of my story. I saw His provision as He prepared my heart for a moment that would've left me feeling completely alone. I'm thankful He permitted me to be in a place of learning to trust Him within the pain I was experiencing.

Learning to trust God during any type of grief isn't an easy thing; it's not meant to be. It's a process that brings us fully surrendered before our Heavenly Father. It's trusting in what He will do, no matter what. This week, take the time to journal through the seasons you had to trust God in grief, waiting, or uncertainty. Let this be a reminder of God's faithfulness!

Lord, as life seems to move between the rails of joy and grief, I pray to have a heart that trusts in you like Daniel. God, many things in my life pose as a distraction, temptation, or pain. God, help me see that not only was it not supposed to be this way, but you also didn't design us to carry the weight of hardship. Lord, I pray for continued growth in my faith and steadfastness that comes with maturity in trusting you during all seasons of my life. In Jesus' name, amen.

thoughts

DON'T DODGE THE HARD STUFF

"My son, if you receive my words and
treasure up my commandments with you,
making your ear attentive to wisdom
and inclining your heart to understanding."
Proverbs 2:1-2

Dodging the hard stuff was a constant theme in my life; I rarely wanted to welcome the light into the dark places that needed attention. I chose to either place the blame elsewhere or pass off what I was dealing with as not a big deal. The problem with this way of living, especially as Christ-followers, is that we are commanded to bring all things to the light, seek wisdom, and seek understanding.

We see this command shared in one of my favorite books of the Bible, the book of Ephesians. "But all things become visible when they are exposed by the light, for everything that becomes visible is light." Ephesians 5:13-14. This alone reminds us that when the darkened places of our hearts are not being tended, there is no way for healing, no place for wisdom.

When I finally realized the importance of this, I unpacked the hard things and brought them before the Lord. This led me to want to study the words "inclining" and "attentive." These two words became the desired posture of my heart; I was listening and leaning in. We have no choice but to lean in and listen to what God is teaching us. How else can we experience His light and restoration without these? When we lean into His truth, listen to His wisdom, and obediently take the hard things to the Lord, He not only restores us, but He uses it to teach us more about who He is.

I want to share two people from scripture who didn't dodge the hard things, but brought everything to the heart of God in prayer.

Hannah - trusting God for a baby (1 Samuel 1:10-11)
"She was deeply distressed and prayed to the Lord and wept bitterly.

And she vowed a vow and said, 'O Lord of hosts, if you will indeed look on the affliction of your servant and remember me and not forget your servant, but will give to your servant a son, then I will give him to the Lord all the days of his life, and no razor shall touch his head.'"

Nehemiah - desiring to return to his desolate homeland (Nehemiah 1:5-11)

He prayed: "O Lord God of Heaven, the great and awesome God who keeps covenant and steadfast love with those who love him and keep his commandments, let your ear be attentive and your eyes open, to hear the prayer of your servant that I now pray before you day and night for the people of Israel your servants, confessing the sins of the people of Israel, which we have sinned against you. Even I and my father's house have sinned. We have acted very corruptly against you and have not kept the commandments, statutes, and rules you commanded your servant, Moses. Remember the word that you commanded your servant, Moses, saying, 'If you are unfaithful, I will scatter you among the peoples, but if you return to me and keep my commandments and do them, though your outcasts are in the uttermost parts of heaven, from there I will gather them and bring them to the place that I have chosen, to make my name dwell there.' They are your servants and your people, whom you have redeemed by your great power and by your strong hand. O Lord, let your ear be attentive to the prayers of your servant, and to the prayer of your servants who delight to fear your name, and give success to your servant today, and grant him mercy in the sight of this man."

These examples seem incredibly different, but both Hannah and Nehemiah found themselves with the same heart posture, fully surrendered to their Heavenly Father, in need of His wisdom, grace, and understanding. The Lord desires this for you and me, too. He desires we turn to Him with hearts, ready and willing to work on the difficult things.

You and I will always be a work-in-progress on this side of Heaven; we can't forget that. We are not perfect. God is. Because He loves us, He wants to sanctify us, grow us, and draw us closer to Him. Let us not miss out on these moments of sanctification, and addressing the hard stuff, just because we'd rather sit in the comfort of complacency. I pray as we stop dodging the hard things and continue bringing them to the Lord, we will gain a deeper understanding of the heart of our Heavenly Father.

This week, carve out time to write the hard stuff you're dodging. Bring everything before the Lord and start seeking His Word as you unpack all that needs healing. Allow His light to permeate the dark, hardened places.

Lord, help me come to you with the hard things in my life. Remind me you desire me to live in your freedom. As I learn your word, I pray my heart will be filled with the truths that help me grow in wisdom.
In Jesus' name, amen.

thoughts

GREATER THAN MY TEMPTATION

"No temptation has overtaken you that
is not common to man. God is faithful, and He will
not let you be tempted beyond your ability;
but with the temptation, He will also provide
the way of escape, that you may be able to endure it."
1 Corinthians 10:13

A few years ago, I went through a season of intense healing from a few weighty sin issues. Thanks be to God! I want to tell you, though, that these sin issues were far more than just a distraction–somehow, they created a snowball effect that convinced me they were part of who I was. I'd concluded that there was no way of escape.

I'm not sure when I first came across 1 Corinthians 10:13 has been underlined in my Bible since 2013, which gives a good indication of the timeline. This was right around the time I started to press into my sinful temptations. Paul penned this scripture as he addressed idolatry and the things that take our eyes off the Lord. We find here a promise from the Lord that there is and always will be a way to escape from our sinful desires, but this way is only found in Christ.

I can vividly remember crying out to the Lord in this season of my life, praying, "God, help me see you as bigger than my temptation." I knew God was greater than anything I would face here on earth. But I finally saw firsthand what idols and temptations do; they cause tension between God's desires for us and the desires of our flesh. So, we have to address our temptations head on with the Lord and ask the questions, "What takes my eyes off the Father?" and "Where do I feel the most tension with my fleshly desires?"

Here's the good news. As we walk in the conviction of handing over our idols and temptations, we walk in the beauty of our God gifted escape plan. An escape plan that will challenge, change, and shape the way we see God and ourselves. You might wonder, where is this escape plan penned? You can find it in Isaiah 9:6. The promise of the long-awaited Savior's coming. Jesus, the Son of God, would come, die, be raised from the dead, ascended into Heaven, and have the authority on His shoulders.

Jesus is the escape plan. Because of His life, we were given the Holy Spirit to guide, direct, and protect us. This escape plan stirs up conviction in our hearts as we live out the process of abiding deeper in Christ. Our escape plan from temptation is the immovable guide we have deep within our hearts. Jesus promised us in John 16:13, "When the Spirit of Truth comes, it will guide you into all truth, for He will not speak on His own authority, but whatever He hears, He will speak, and He will declare to you the things that are to come."

God will always be faithful to lead us out of sin and away from temptations. We just have to be willing to follow Him. We have to live out the truth, knowing that He is greater than anything we face. Jesus came because God knew there needed to be an escape plan from our sin, which includes the temptations we face and the idols we create.

This week, take time to sit in prayer and look back at your life. Journal about the things God has freed you from and the things you're praying for freedom in. Thank Him for our promised way of escape–a plan designed for you and me to live in perfect union with Him. As the Holy Spirit stirs up convictions in your heart about what takes your eyes off Him, lay them at the foot of the cross. Trust His heart, trust His leading, and trust His plan.

Jesus, thank you for being the example to us of not giving into temptation. God, I pray I would see you always as greater than any temptation that comes my way. When my flesh feels the pull to go against you, I ask Lord that you would place your word on my tongue. I pray for awareness that senses when the Holy Spirit reveals to me that temptation is coming and that I would turn from it immediately.

In Jesus' name, amen.

thoughts

HE IS IN OUR MIDST

"God is in the midst of her;
she shall not be moved;
God will help her when morning dawns."
Psalm 46:5

I love the reminder that God is our fortress, our safe place. He breaks brows and defeats our enemies. He calls us to be still and promises us He is in our midst. I was captivated by God's promise in Psalm 46:5: "God is in the midst of her; she shall not be moved; God will help her when morning dawns." This was being spoken of God's treasured place, Israel. He promises these very things to you and me, too. Jesus tells us in Matthew 28 that "He is with us always to the very end of the age." This means He is our everyday help and sustainer.

Isn't it beautiful the way God speaks straight to our hearts through His Word? He gave us an entire book out of His love for us to understand Him more deeply. He shows us how to live for Him, love like Him, and lead people to Him. This book humbles us, convicts us, and brings redemption to our souls. He never sleeps nor slumbers. He never overlooks you for another task.

Personally, as a wife, mama, and person pursuing a ministry on my heart, I can quickly become overwhelmed with the duties I'm called to live out within the roles I've been given. I sometimes find myself asking, "How can I do it all?" and "How can I do all the God-given assignments well?". The simple answer is this: we don't, He does. We know this from His Word. He makes this concrete for us. We can't do anything well apart from the grace and goodness of God. We, as fallen humans, cannot complete every task in our strength.

I think of everything Israel was going through when this particular Psalm was written and of all the redemption God had in store for His land. Any work God begins, He will faithfully bring it to completion. Rest assured, all the good things that flow out of you and me are because of Him.

Psalm 46 was written by someone who felt overwhelmed by the things they had been facing, yet they were completely secure in who God is. The author knew God was present, trustworthy, and wouldn't step outside of His character. He trusted that within his stillness and submission, God would move. God would be the Protector. God would complete what He had begun. This is precisely where you and I need to be today: secure in who God is, knowing He is trustworthy, and knowing He will never step outside of His character.

So, perhaps your daily life and responsibilities look like a life you can't possibly keep up with, or maybe it just doesn't look like what you'd hoped it would, you can still rest in the unwavering truth that God is with you, He is sustaining you, and He is working on our behalf. You can trust that if there is any part of your life unaligned with Him, He will bring that to the surface through conviction of the Holy Spirit.

My prayer for you and me today is that we will desire to be still, we will learn to submit more freely, and we will live lives that put on display the truth that we know God is in our midst. As this week unfolds, ask the Lord to show you what areas of your life you need to surrender to Him. Are there specific tasks in your routine that you feel are yours and not God's? The more freely we come to Him, the more willing we will be to make Him the center of our lives.

Jesus, help me see you during my everyday schedule. Help me have a heart that leans into the truth of your word as I learn to trust you with where you have me. Lead me to the things you've purposed for me and help me hand over the things you've not asked me to carry.
In Jesus' name, amen.

thoughts

ARE WE COUNTING THE COST?

"But He was pierced for our transgressions,
He was crushed for our iniquities;
the punishments that brought us peace
was on Him, and by His wounds we are healed."
Isaiah 53:5

While reading the book, *In His Image* by Jen Wilkin, there was a chapter all about grace and the cost for us to receive this ultimate gift. Since becoming a Christian, I have wrestled with the words to describe how passionately I feel about God's grace and why we must look at it as something sacred. It shouldn't be something we just pull out of a deck of cards to lay on the table; it's not a word we should throw around or allow to be watered down by the world. God's grace, which came from Jesus dying on the cross, gives us the gift of eternal life. "By His grace, we are saved" (Ephesians 2:8-9) and "by His wounds, we are healed" (Isaiah 53:5).

I want you to prayerfully sit with these words from Dietrich Bonhoeffer the same way I did.

"Cheap grace is the preaching of forgiveness without requiring repentance, baptism without church discipline, Communion without confession, absolution without personal confession. Cheap grace is grace without discipleship, grace without the cross, grace without Jesus Christ, living and incarnate. Costly grace is the treasure hidden in the field; for the sake of it, a man will go and sell all that he has. It is the pearl of great price to buy, which the merchant will sell all his goods. It is the kingly rule of Christ, for whose sake a man will pluck out the eye which causes him to stumble; it is the call of Jesus Christ at which the disciple leaves his nets and follows him. Costly grace is the gospel which must be sought again and again, the gift which must be asked for, the door at which a man must knock. Such grace is costly because it calls us to follow, and it is grace because it calls us to follow Jesus Christ. It is costly because it costs a man his life, and it is grace because it gives a man the only true life. It is costly

because it condemns sin and grace because it justifies the sinner. Above all, it is costly because it cost God the life of his Son: "Ye were bought at a price," and what has cost God much cannot be cheap for us. Above all, it is grace because God did not reckon his Son too dear a price to pay for our life but delivered Him up for us. Costly grace is the Incarnation of God."
- Dietrich Bonhoeffer

The grace we receive calls us to count the cost. It calls us to know the whole truth about Jesus and why He had to come. He died in our place so that we could have the gift of eternal life, that we could be filled with the Holy Spirit, and He died so we could have a relationship with the One who created us. This is something so unlike anything else. Grace is something we certainly don't deserve. Our sin sent Jesus to the cross, but God so loved the world He gave up His one and only Son for us. (John 3:16)

The next time you're in a season of needing grace, which we know is daily, join me in pursuit of asking the Lord to help us count the cost of His grace. To help us see that there was a price for our freedom in Christ. I never want to end up in a place where the thought of the cross doesn't cause me to pause. So maybe you're asking how do I ensure I don't get to that place? We keep our minds on the cross and stay steadfast in His word. We fix our eyes on Jesus and the grace that His life has given us. We can't unlearn the truth, but we can certainly let it become dull. The grace of God is a gift that shouldn't lessen in value over time but should grow in significance as a reminder of why we need Him and how faithful He is.

This week take time to study God's grace—what did it cost our Heavenly Father to make it possible that we could spend eternity with Him? Write what you find as you study and how you see the heart of God through the gift of His Son to us.

Lord, help me remember the cost of grace today, tomorrow, and each day that follows until you call me home. Thank you for what you did on the cross and for standing in my place. The cost was so great, and I'm so thankful for the freedom I have in you. In Jesus' name, amen.

thoughts

WON'T HE DO IT?

"Now may the God of peace Himself sanctify
you completely, and may your whole spirit
be kept blameless at the coming of our Lord Jesus Christ.
He who calls you is faithful; He will surely do it."
1 Thessalonians 5:23-24

1 Thessalonians 5:24 is a current favorite among many Christians, and it deems God faithful to fulfill all the dreams we've got in our hearts because "He will surely do it." Well, praise God, Paul clears up this misunderstanding in the verse before it. He's talking about sanctification, not all the things we want in this life. He starts by praying, "now may the God of peace Himself sanctify you completely." This means that as we live our lives for the Lord, we choose to submit to His mission, which means we are choosing to sit under the authority of God the Father and His sanctification—and yes, won't He do it!

I promise you; the very things God has called you to do for His Kingdom are also the same things He will use to sanctify you. Being on a mission for the Lord is a beautiful process of excitement for the Kingdom but hard work of flushing out the flesh. Let's look at Paul as an example. We see the entire trajectory of his life change because of his submission to God. Through this, we see an incredible work the Lord did in Paul's heart as he went from living for himself to living on behalf of God's plans.

Paul's desires aligned with God's desires because he understood the process. He understood he needed to know God, be on a mission to make Him known, and desire to look more like Him (which happens only through sanctification). The same goes for us, too. As we learn God's voice through His Word and grow in following His lead, we will see our desires shift to align with what He commands of us. This will cause our hearts to celebrate the stirrings of conviction and see God's sanctification as a gift.

1 Thessalonians 5:23-24 gives us the provision we need to remember that this life is not to be lived on our own accord. Our life isn't a "wing it" project; our life was created by God Almighty with a purpose. Because of this, we learn that we have to lay down our fleshly desires and ambitions to obediently choose to do the things God leads us to. Sometimes the "thing" God is asking us to choose will look outlandish, other times, it's a small ordinary act of obedience.

God wants us to live a life that celebrates and glorifies all He's doing through our sanctification journey. There is no fleshly desire or plan that can refine us the way God's sanctification will. Let us stand firm in what we know to be true: we must live tethered to His will and His way. Let us not fall prey to any other desires than what God wants for us.

This week, during your quiet time, ask the Lord to lead you to places in His word that will build up your faith when you need to stand firm against the desires of the flesh and twisted messages that will try to pull you away from Him. Find peace and comfort knowing God is faithful in the call and He will do through you what He desires; however, we know that it won't always be pleasing to the flesh. We must follow His Mission, His way, for Him and His Kingdom.

Heavenly Father, I pray I will always allow your word to master me. I pray I will always acknowledge that my life isn't to please me but glorify and honor you. Help me see that on days when the sanctification process is hard. Lord, remind me of 1 Thessalonians 5:23-24, that you promise to sanctify us because you LOVE us. And Lord, when the world tries to manipulate your word to suit their agenda, I pray for a strong faith that stands the test of time. May my heart always be for Christ and The Kingdom. In Jesus' name, amen.

thoughts

HIS PERFECTION AND OUR
NEED FOR HIS GRACE

"They still bear fruit in old age; they are ever full of sap and
green, to declare that the LORD is upright; he is my rock,
and there is no unrighteousness in him."
Psalm 92: 14-15

"The closer our relationship is with the Lord, the more aware we are of our deep need for Him," my pastor said during a Sunday morning sermon. And while I'm sure I've heard something like that many times over the last nine years, it stirred something up in my heart in a new way. It caused me to reflect and see that what he said was most certainly true in my life and probably true of yours, too. Over the last nine years of knowing Christ, I know that day by day, I've become more stunningly aware of God's perfection and holiness and how deeply in need of His grace I am.

Psalm 92 proclaims, "To declare that the Lord is upright; He is my rock, and there is no unrighteousness in Him." This verse confirmed precisely what my pastor had said. Our Heavenly Father is the definition of righteousness. Becoming more aware of our need for Him is a pivotal point in our walk because, within this truth, we can see that His perfection and righteousness shatter the sin inside of us and slashes through the enemy's tactics. Here's something I want to point out to you; God's perfection is part of His grace for us. Without God's perfection, there is no need for grace to be given because a covering for our sin can't come from anything less than perfect. Isn't that amazing? Within the perfect holiness and love of God, He allowed us to become right with Him, knowing we are unrighteous.

I remember the first time I noticed that my sin equaled a consequence. I finally felt accountable for the pain I inflicted on myself through my sin because I turned away from what God desired for me. At that moment, I now knew the weight of my sin. I just didn't know what to do with it. Grace was about to eclipse my barren soul. I look back at that younger version of me, standing empty-handed, yet on the brink of a life fully surrendered to the Lord, and I wish I could tell her...

"Everything about God is perfect. His love, His law, His Word, and His character. You've been running from this for so long but take hold of God's pursuit of you. He is sheer perfection, perfectly righteous, and just. God loves you so much, even in this moment of brokenness, and He's brought you to this moment of seeing the detriments of your sin. While I know you want to be free from the ache of your choices, you're going to seek to understand the price that Jesus paid for you on the cross and what the true meaning of grace over your life is. Because without the knowledge of why God sent His son and where grace came from, you won't understand how sacred this relationship with the Lord is and how desperate we need our Savior."

For us to get a glimpse into the perfect, righteous heart of our Father, we must know and go to where the deepest form of love was shown to us: Jesus on the cross. We can never lose sight of this image, and we can't afford to skip over this part of the story. The cross is just as crucial as the resurrection. You can't celebrate the grace of God without knowing about Jesus's death on the cross. We can't afford to overlook these details; it's too costly. These are the details that changed our lives forever. Our perfect Heavenly Father sent His perfect Son, Jesus, to offer us grace and mercy. I pray as you walk with Christ that you not only remember this but share this: we are imperfect people who have to grow in awareness of our deep need for our Savior and always seek the heart of our Father.

This week ask the Lord to give you eyes to see your blind spots, dig deeper into the parts of your life that suppress receiving His grace. Also, pray that the Lord would lay on your heart someone to share His message with.

Lord, today I ask one thing - help me to see my deep need for your grace. I pray that not one day goes by that I forget how much I need you. Thank you for the mercy, grace, and love that you show me daily. In Jesus' name, amen.

thoughts

week twenty-nine
THE FREEDOM KEEPS COMING

"Perfect love drives out fear."
1 John 4:18

The Lord wasn't just giving a suggestion when He said to be careful of what we see and hear. I think many of us can attest to this. Years of concrete memories from our earlier days linger in our minds. Unfortunately, these memories will either breathe life and His light into our bones, or they'll be used as ammunition for the evil one. A few months ago, I sat in bed and couldn't shake horrible scenes from movies and videos I had seen in my teen years. As I wrestled and prayed, I felt compelled to write them all out on paper, including the awful thoughts and feelings they were plaguing me with. It was time to hand these over to Jesus. As I read them aloud to the Lord and stumbled over tears, my heart was overcome by 1 John 4:18, "Perfect love drives out fear."

I'm sure you've had some of these challenging days. The ones that are laced with painful memories or visions of things you saw or words you'd heard. I'm sure you, too, have wondered why or how these keep coming back up? This question was finally answered for me that day in my bed. We have to bring all these memories to the Lord, not just squander them when they arise. The Lord tells us in 2 Corinthians 10:5, "to take all thoughts captive and make them obedient to Christ." We have to remember this truth and that His perfect love will drive out fear. His perfect love has the power to cleanse our minds when we bring our painful memories to Him. We can't forget the freedom we were promised in Christ the day we accepted Him. Freedom in Christ means He continues to lead us into more freedom day by day.

I'll never forget dropping the shreds of that piece of paper in the trash with all the fear-filling, painful things on it. I walked away and let out praise to the Lord, "You just keep making me free." Friend, His freedom doesn't stop coming. How amazing is that? "Whom the Son sets free, he is free indeed." (John 8:36) This means every single day; we can experience more freedom as we bring these burdens before Him.

129

I learned a few things that day. One, that fear and His perfect love can't reside in the same places of the heart. Truth, love, grace, and mercy all reside in the light. Two, it's our duty as believers to lean in, listen to His voice, and bring our memories, fear, and pain to the light so that His love can pierce through them. Three, we must stop squandering what continues to linger in our minds, and shift to prayerfully bring everything before the Lord.

I praise the Lord often for that beautiful, sunny Friday morning. I saw firsthand, the importance of daily pursuing the freedom found in Christ, and I want you to know He desires the very same freedom for you.

As you end your reading today, I pray that you know the Lord wants to walk you through whatever is plaguing you with fear and pain. Write it on paper, read it aloud, and lay it down at His feet, just as He has commanded. I can promise His perfect love is covering you, and it is only through Him that we will experience a heart anchored in everlasting freedom.

As you walk into the week, let 1 John 4:18 rule in your heart. Take time to sit with the Lord and ask Him to show you the areas in your life that are driven by fear and pain. Pray for His redemption and restoration to fill these places in your heart.

Heavenly Father, I pray that I never forget where our freedom comes from and that it is laced with your love and mercy. Help me to live a life that honors you, by walking in this gift you've given us, and I pray that in my obedience, others can be stewarded to experience this gift too.
In Jesus' name, amen.

thoughts

RESCUE AND HONOR

"Because he holds fast to me in love, I will deliver him;
I will protect him because he knows my name. When he
calls me, I will answer him; I will be with him in trouble;
I will rescue him and honor him. With long life,
I will satisfy him and show him my salvation."
Psalm 91:14-16

This Scripture above hangs on the wall of my son's room. Cam knows them as "God's Words." Let me just say this before we dig in: there is nothing sweeter in this world than hearing your almost-four-year-old know where these truths come from. Before bed, he'll sometimes tell us what those words say, "He protects me, He answers me, and He saves me my whole life." While the sweetness lingers in the air, there is a deep sense of peace, knowing he already knows this about the God we serve. It reminds me daily why you and I need to always remember this promise, too.

Psalm 91 is one of my most favorite passages of Scripture. Verses 14-16 specifically call us to obedience while also getting to experience the fulfillment of God's promise over our life. It points our hearts back to the truth of who God is and why we need Him. It calls us to hold fast to Him, to call out to Him, and to trust in His salvation, just like the sweet paraphrase spoken in Cam's toddler voice: to protect us, answer us, and keep us safe. I wonder, though, how often do we let the things in our day-to-day take our eyes off the promises God has given us? Personally, it can feel so easy to blame my lack of obedience due to being tired, worn down, or weary from carrying my own burdens. Does this sound like you, too?

When I think of the day-to-day feelings and tasks taking my eyes off Jesus, I immediately picture when Jesus called Peter to step out of the boat and walk on water with Him in Matthew 14. Peter stepped out in faith, fully confident, with eyes on Jesus. To find himself only to be underwater moments later. Why? Because he quickly took his gaze off trusting His Savior. He got caught in the fleeting feelings that come with this world. (Matthew 14:30-31)

Doesn't this sound like us? We start our days with our eyes on Jesus. We are ready for what He has for us, and like Peter, we confidently step out of the boat. When suddenly, the fight with our spouse happens, our parents suddenly are ill, our children haven't gone five minutes without an argument we had to diffuse, or our friends passively dismissed a critical conversation we needed to have. Somehow, these murky minutes of our days have us sinking just like Peter.

We can see in our sinking that we've allowed our situations to take our eyes off Jesus and the promises He's given us. I pray this is a reminder to you to keep your eyes focused on the Lord. Lean on Him and delight in Him as you walk throughout your days. Remember that each day is an assignment from the Lord. Look to Him and His provision for how you're to endure it!

This week, as you start your days with your eyes on Jesus, ask Him to keep your eyes fixed there. As you sit with Him in prayer, ask Him to reveal what's taking your eyes off Him. Write all that comes to mind on paper, pray through them, and ask for the Lord's guidance as you live out removing what's been catching your gaze. Write His promises on your heart and hold fast to them.

Lord, some days it seems so difficult to remember how faithful you are. Help me this week as I lean into becoming more aware of you in the moments that try to take my eyes off you. Help me be a woman of great faith because I recognize what an amazing God I serve.
In Jesus' name, amen.

thoughts

week thirty-one
HOLY BOLDNESS

"Now, when they saw the boldness of Peter
and John and perceived that they were
uneducated, common men, they were astonished.
And they recognized that they had been with Jesus."
Acts 4:13

Holy Boldness. We, as Christians, desire to get this right. Still, we often find ourselves in the messy middle of intensity and irritation or hesitancy and holding back. We try to make conversations happen and will our way over God's leading. In Acts 4, the Lord stewards our hearts in a sweet yet bold way. He shows us that fleshly boldness is not the same as holy boldness. Holy boldness makes believers and non-believers want to lean in, not because it's intimidating or abrasive, but because God's truth captivates a wondering heart.

When I study the Word of God, one of the things I always take note of is scriptures with repetitive words, promises, and phrases. This is something I challenge you to do as well. In Acts 4:13, Paul made it clear why we're called to be bold in our faith, and He also made it very clear how we can only do this when we're filled with and led by the Holy Spirit.

As we study the Word, we can also see that the Lord has called us to pursue boldness with a holy perspective, not an earthly one. Through the lens of Jesus's life, we see that He had a very intentional way about how He approached people: God-led and open-armed. While we're not going to always get this right, we have to take note of the posture of Christ's heart. Open, not closed. Willing, not resistant. This call to boldness is a challenge to the flesh and one the Lord uses to prune us to make us look more like Him.

For me, boldness typically comes out in the form of a conversation. Early last year, the Lord stirred something in my heart to ask a friend that would typically be awkward to mention, but I knew it was from Him. I'm sure you've found yourself there: wanting to say what God has stirred up in your heart but also feeling your flesh wish to hold back. But God moved, and I obeyed. This conversation ended up shedding light on a darkened place in my friend's life, not because of my words, but because of obediently stepping out in the boldness of the Holy Spirit.

You see, our words steward people. God's Word changes people. This means when we speak God's Word, it permeates places the enemy wants to keep locked up and darkened. There's too high of a cost for us to hide behind a hesitant faith. Boldness in Christ will take us from a faith of hesitancy to a faith built on solid ground.

How can you be bold this week as you step out into the world that is so desperate for His light? Spend some time praying over the verses from Acts and see where His heart leads you. Ask yourself, how will you live with a less hesitant faith today? In what small ways can you obey the Lord by serving someone who doesn't know Him?

Jesus, I pray for an awakening of my heart that causes me to be bold for the Kingdom. I pray that my heart would move when you say "GO." Remove in me anything that delays obedience to what you're asking. God help me be sensitive to your Spirit as I walk hand in hand with it. In Jesus' name, amen.

thoughts

KINGDOM EYES

"So shall my word be that goes out from my mouth;
it shall not return to me empty, but it shall
accomplish that which I purpose, and shall succeed
in the thing for which I sent it."
Isaiah 55:11

"Clear eyes, full hearts, can't lose." This is a common saying I see floating around. I wonder what would happen if we changed it to "Kingdom eyes and Christ-filled hearts, can't lose." This hinges on the promise that no matter what we face in this life, we know who we live for, and that Christ has the final victory. If this was how we chose to see the world, I can only imagine what would happen on behalf of the Kingdom of God through His people. I pray you know the importance of this, too.

The Lord often reminds me to have "Kingdom eyes" when I find myself wrestling with people getting this life so twisted. When I'm looking through the lens of my own vantage point, I can get overwhelmed by the rampant wickedness we see in this world. I'm sure I'm in good company here. Through this, though, the Lord has taken me back to the truth that conviction and reliance on Him is all in the choice of the person; and that my job as the believer is to guide and direct these people to the truth, knowing I can't change them, but God can.

I spent a chunk of time recently reading through the book of Habakkuk. This is a short, intensely packed book of the Bible, one that if you may not have read before, your heart will be better for it once you do. We see God clearly respond to Habakkuk's questioning of why people are wicked. "They are dreaded and fearsome; their justice and dignity go forth from themselves." Habakkuk 1:7 These men are apart from God. Their hearts are driven by the hate, spite, and earthly strength found within their godless soul. Their hearts are wandering the world, looking for something to fill it. This example clarifies what happens when we live by the might of man and not by letting God rule and reign over our hearts.

One of the greatest reminders God ever gave me happened when I was looking to His Word about having a Kingdom perspective and taking it one step further by wanting to genuinely live it out. He reminded me that many of the people living for themselves are in some ways just like the unsaved version of me. Prideful, snarky, ruthless, and just downright disobedient. I need to look at these people through the lens of God's desires for their hearts and how I needed to be stewarded to truth in that season.

Isaiah 55:11 tells us God's Word will never return void. This is what we must remember as we get placed in front of the people of this world; the prideful, the snarky, the ruthless, and the downright disobedient. We steward the lost souls to the truth by speaking it. Imagine what can happen in the hearts of those around us if we speak God's Word each time the opportunity presents itself. Friend, if we can see from our Kingdom perspective someone whose heart needs restoring by the Father, we must share the unchanging Word that saves and severs the heart of stone.

As you and I live a life centered on Christ, shifting our perspective to one for the Kingdom, and seek to grow in the knowledge of His Word that never returns void; our hearts become tethered tightly to His, and through that, we get the honor of inviting others to have that same relationship with the Lord.

I want to wrap us up with this today, picture a tetherball and its poll. The ball can only go so far before winding itself up and resting against where it belongs. This is us in Christ. We are tethered to the Lord, and we will always end up back at the foot of the cross through God's grace and mercy over us. But it's a different story for the people who are apart from God, their hearts hang on to nothing but a murky world. Their souls aren't anchored in the truth from the One who saves.

So, join me this week (and all the days we have left on this earth), and let's point the hearts of those around us to the truth and heart of God. Journal the names of those you want to specifically pray for to come to know the Lord; it could be someone in your workplace, a younger woman who just started coming to church, or perhaps it's someone within your four walls at home—make it a point to serve and love these people boldly.

Lord, you teach us to look at this life through the lens of eternity.
I desire to get this right. My perspective can be easily shifted, but I
know as I grow in my awareness of you and your Spirit, I will be more
diligent in seeing the world the way you call us. Help me begin each day
by asking for your vision, clarity, and desire to live like you.
In Jesus' name, amen.

thoughts

week thirty three

HOLY ENDURANCE > HUSTLE CULTURE

"It is for discipline that you have to endure.
God is treating you as sons. For what son is there
whom his father does not discipline?"
Hebrews 12:7

Hebrews 12 has been a favorite part of Scripture for me since I became a believer. I loved that it pointed me to all that God wanted to do in and through my life. It was a part of Scripture that pierced my heart and gave me an understanding of why the Lord disciplines His children.

Over the last few years, we've watched the "self-help, hustle culture" invade the walls of Christianity. These messages, which seem intoxicating, have caught like wildfire within the hearts of our women in the church. This has caused a holy fire within me. I no longer can sit idle and watch women of God be swayed by the perversion of God's Word. The new "culture" has tried to deceivingly grab onto the rails of Hebrews 12 and mask itself as truth. All while diminishing the true gospel message and elevating oneself. To my sisters in Christ reading this today, I promise you these false messages being pushed on you by the world are filled with hopelessness. They are filled with the lies that you can be the hero of your own story when you can't be; only Jesus can.

There is something incredible tucked in Hebrews 12 that often gets overlooked and will never be talked about within the message of the hustle culture. In verse 10, we see it begins talking about discipline from a parent's perspective but then reveals to us that the discipline we experience from God, the perfect Father, is an invitation to His holiness. "For they disciplined us for a short time as it seemed best to them, but He disciplines us for our good, that we may share his holiness." God desires for us to experience His holiness. Ponder that with me. That is the heart of our Father.

Holy Endurance is an endurance set in God's strength, not our own. Within this endurance, we're called to accountability and obedience to do what God asks of us. It flips the *message of me* on its head and shows us why we need less of who we are and more of who God is. Verse 15 gives us a clear reminder as to

145

why we need to cling to the endurance found in Christ and not the frailty of man. "See to it that no one fails to obtain the grace of God; that no 'root of bitterness springs up and causes trouble, and by it many become defiled." We see here that as followers of Christ, we are held accountable to see that no one fails to obtain the grace of God. Which means we must point hearts away from any message that teaches otherwise.

The world of "self-help, hustle culture" hurries hearts, and it most certainly doesn't offer the message of God's grace. I pray that we write the words that finish Hebrews 12:28 on our hearts: "Therefore let us be grateful for receiving a kingdom that cannot be shaken, and thus let us offer to God acceptable worship, with reverence and awe." I pray you will join me in living our lives in a posture that doesn't sidestep experiencing the fullness of God and what He desires for us. I pray that we can discern the false teachings of this world and hold fast to God's Word as we keep our eyes fixed on Him.

This week, as you spend time with the Lord, pray for the conviction of your heart if you've been caught up in hustle culture. Ask the Lord if you've been leaning too heavily on self-help messages and not Him as sustainer. Be honest and let the work of the Holy Spirit lead your heart.

> Lord, thank you for your living Word. I'm so grateful that you
> give us discipline and instruction. It shows how much you love me
> and care for me. Lord, help me always keep my eyes on you
> and the mission you have set before me. In Jesus' name, amen.

thoughts

week thirty four

OUR MESS DOESN'T
NEGATE HIS GOODNESS

"But when anything is exposed by the light,
it becomes visible."
Ephesians 5:13

Have you ever wondered, *how can God love the messy parts of me?* I have, too. I'm sure many of us have also found ourselves thinking, "the messy parts of me are hard, they feel unmanageable, and at times make my world feel dark." As I walked through an emotionally messy season, the Lord stirred this on my heart one evening, "I love you where you are, but I love you too much to leave things in the dark." I felt complete peace in this moment knowing the Lord was ushering this broken part of my heart to His light. Ephesians 5:13 says, "But when anything is exposed by the light, it becomes visible." God used this Scripture to pierce through my flesh and put His living Word on display.

As women, bringing things to the light can be difficult. We like to be seen as tidy, cleaned up, in order, and with our joy tank filled to the brim. But can I be honest with you? Living in the false reality of trying to look perfect has unfortunately overflowed into the way we approach God. This way of living has cost us something. It costs us the grace and mercy we experience because Jesus went to the cross. Our heavenly Father sent Jesus to the cross because we can't attain perfection.

The Lord shows us repeatedly in Scripture that our mess doesn't negate His goodness. We see this on display through the lives of David and Bathsheba (2 Samuel 11), Rahab the prostitute (Joshua 2), and the Apostle Paul, who once lived for killing Christians (Acts 22). While God never desires for our lives to be a mess or for us to partake in sin, by His grace and mercy for us, He draws us closer as we bring our failures to Him. The redemption we experience through the gift of Jesus is one of the greatest blessings we have on this side of eternity.

I may not know what your "mess" is or looks like, but I can promise you that Jesus wants you to lay it down before Him. He wants you to surrender every facet of your life. Isn't there so much freedom in that? He not only desires a relationship with you, but He wants to change the parts of you that desperately need light and life breathed into them. He wants to reveal Himself to you and use you for the Kingdom.

Friend, I wish I could sit next to you today, hold your hand, look you in the eyes and share this promise with you: our walk with the Lord will not be easy. He loves you right where you are, mess and all, but He loves you too much to leave you this way. Our Father wants you to be sanctified in truth and refined by the holy fire.

This week, carve out time to be in prayer with the Lord over the mess (es) in your life. Look to His Word for wisdom and understanding as you walk through the redemption, He offers you. Choose surrender, choose the growth that comes from walking out your convictions, and trust God's heart as He leads you.

Lord, help me seek your face first and foremost, no matter what my circumstances look like. Reveal the parts of me I've hidden away or buried. I desire you to heal these places in my heart, Lord. Shine your light brightly into them, expose them, remove them, and lead me to the freedom you desire for me. In Jesus' name, amen.

thoughts

HOLD FAST TO WHAT IS GOOD

"And let us not grow weary of doing good, for in
due season we will reap, if we do not give up."
Galatians 6:9

Over the last several years, God has shown me how importance of, "hold fast
to what is good". These words come from 1 Thessalonians 5:21. This scripture is
one that keeps me looking to the Lord throughout my marriage and to honor the
commitment we made.

Culture has swiftly ushered in the lie that we should only hold fast to what is
easy or most mutually beneficial. The definition of *good* has been deluded into
something that looks more like a business transaction. You do for me, and I'll do
for you. It's no wonder people don't uphold the commitments they make. We see
this on the daily, failing marriages, friendships, businesses, and churches falling
apart due to lack of commitment. This has left me wanting to understand true
commitment from the Lord's perspective: what does the Word say, how did Jesus
live it out, and how can we live committed to all that the Lord has called us to?

First, we need to begin with God's covenants. Through His covenants, we can
grasp the importance of honoring the commitments we've made.

"In form, a covenant is an agreement between two people and involves promises
on the part of each to the other. The concept of a covenant between God and His
people is one of the central themes of the Bible. In the Biblical sense, a covenant
implies much more than a contract or a simple agreement between two parties.
The word for "covenant" in the Old Testament also provides additional insight
into the meaning of this important idea. It comes from a Hebrew root word that
means "to cut." This explains the strange custom of two people passing through
the cut bodies of slain animals after making an agreement (cf. Jeremiah. 34:18). A
ceremony such as this always accompanied the making of a covenant in the Old
Testament. Sometimes those entering into a covenant shared a meal, such as when
Laban and Jacob made their covenant (Genesis. 31:54)."-David Padfield

Second, how do we see Jesus living out commitment during His ministry on earth.

"And the Word became flesh and dwelt among us, and we have seen his glory, glory as of the only Son from the Father, full of grace and truth." John 1:14

"This is why Jesus lived. To be God's Word — His truth, His instruction, His will — in human flesh. It's as if God is saying, "You want to see the Bible lived correctly? Here's My Son. Watch Him.

The Word became flesh and healed and fed and taught the crowds. The Word showed love and grace to sinners without compromising truth. The Word was a servant to all. Most of all, God's Word in flesh showed us how we can become the Word in flesh.

Jesus lived to establish God's kingdom on earth by doing the King's will. And God wants to extend that kingdom through all of us — not through pursuing power and influence, but by simply doing His will." -Ray Vander Laan

Last, how can we live committed to what has been commanded of us?

We hold fast to what is good in the eyes of the Lord. We seek to obey God and follow His commands. We stay committed to the work of the Great Commission (Matthew 28) as we keep Christ at the center of our life. We stay in step with the Holy Spirit (Galatians 5:25) and we live according to the will of God, not of man (Matthew 4:4).

These three examples show how important commitment is to God and that we should seek to honor the commitments we've made before Him. We need to remember this, "what God has joined together, let no man separate." Do not let the world lure you into the temptation of ease when things get difficult. Look to scripture and hold fast to His goodness. This week, reflect on the commitments you've made before the Lord and pray for a heart that seeks to honor them out of your love for the Lord.

Lord, thank you for another day of new mercies. God, I pray this week my heart would find itself rejoicing in the promise that you'll never not pick me. You chose me from the beginning and you'll keep pursuing my heart forever. Lord, give me the strength when I don't want to follow through my commitments. Lord, help me make the best yes, the one that honors you above all other things. I love you Lord, thank you for your unfailing love. In Jesus' name, amen.

thoughts

week thirty-six
LET'S WRESTLE

"Every branch in me that does not bear fruit,
He takes away; and every branch that does bear fruit,
He prunes, that it may bear more fruit."
John 15:2

Let's *wrestle*. This short phrase has been one that marks many seasons of my faith. Seasons of wrestling are a guarantee on this side of Heaven. Not only are they a guarantee, but they're also necessary for our growth as they bring our fleshly desires, pride-filled hearts, questions, worries, doubts, and fears all to the Lord. These seasons of wrestling give us the ability to watch God work in the places we can find ourselves hiding away. We wrestle with God because we can't be all-knowing or fully grasp what God is doing. We're fallen, we want control, and we want to know the outcomes.

When I picture a wrestling match, I think about the afternoons we spent at my grandparents as a young girl. All of us cousins would end up in one big wrestling match with my dad. They all started differently, but they all ended the same. This is precisely how each season of wrestling plays out in my life with the Lord: it begins differently, but it always ends the same. I come out closer to the Lord, and my heart is changed for the better by His grace.

Wrestling out our questions and concerns with the Lord will be one of the many ways God draws us to a deeper relationship with Him. We'll find ourselves with a deeper faith and a deeper trust in the Lord. There are many places in the Bible where we see people caught in the wrestling match between what God asks of them and what they desire. This makes me think of Nicodemus. He had quite the wrestling match going on inside his heart. So much so that he sought out Jesus in the middle of the night in secrecy.

The story of Nicodemus in John 3:1-15 is so important. Here's a snippet to give you some context:

"Now there was a man of the Pharisees named Nicodemus, a ruler of the Jews. This man came to Jesus by night and said to him, 'Rabbi, we know you are a teacher come from God, for no one can do these signs that you do unless God is with him.' Jesus answered him, 'Truly, truly, I say to you, unless one is born again, he cannot see the kingdom of God.'

I love seeing the character of God's heart through the way Jesus handled Nicodemus. Jesus invited him in, listened to his heart, and shared the truth that would set him free. We can know with complete certainty that we won't be rejected for wrestling; instead, we'll be drawn in as we seek God's heart for understanding.

The work God is doing in our lives will never stop unfolding. The wrestling matches will continue season after season as we grow in refinements. Jesus promises this to us in John 15:2. "Every branch in me that does not bear fruit, He takes away; and every branch that does bear fruit, He prunes, that it may bear more fruit."

Spend time this week journaling about the best things God has taught you in a season of wrestling. Or perhaps you're in one of those seasons now, if so, what do you see the Lord doing?

5 Things God Taught Me in the Wrestling Match

1) A challenging season is always on the horizon, and therefore we must grow and mature in faith so that we can endure while we cling to Christ. (Hebrews 12:2)

2) God can handle our honesty with Him, surrender our words, thoughts, and feelings. (Philippians 4:6)

3) Keep the shield of faith up at all times. (Ephesians 6:16)

4) The Lord wants to reveal Himself to us; He's not hiding. (Psalm 25:14)

5) Hold fast to Him and His Word. (1 Thessalonians 5:21)

Lord, I come to you with a thankful heart that you're my safest place to process things with. I pray as I go through seasons of wrestling, I will always find myself digging into your Word and what you have to say about my struggles. Lord, may I always remember your desire to make yourself known to me. In Jesus' name, amen.

thoughts

week thirty seven

TRIPPED UP AND THE REVEALING OF SIN

"We demolish arguments and every pretension that
sets itself up against the knowledge of God, and we
take captive every thought to make it obedient to Christ."
2 Corinthians 10:5

I can be an extremely reminiscent person within the walls of my own mind. If I come across something attached to a memory, I find myself in the tailspin of yesteryears. This never seemed like an issue to me. I chalked it up to being just part of who I was—a woman who loves details while also having a really great memory. But, in a tough season, these "detailed memories" became heavier than just reminiscing. These memories became a way of escape for me, so I didn't have to face the disappointment I had in my own life. These memories were no longer just tripping me up; they were landing my heart and mind in full-fledged sin.

Perhaps you feel like this isn't a topic you struggle with, or maybe you don't feel like you are one to get tripped up by memories. But we all have discontentment with things, and God wants us to take all those thoughts to Him. Three days before sitting down to write this, the Lord reminded me of a portion of a book that I read some time ago. This life-changing excerpt focused on how I view my memories, daydreams, and areas of discontentment in my life. My prayer is that God uses these words powerfully for you, too.

"Unhindered daydreams can be dangerous if allowed to grow. If not properly aligned with Scripture to hold them accountable or prayed over with godly friends to help keep them in check, these seemingly harmless dreams can turn into a woman's worst nightmare..." We need to be aware. To be vigilant. To take our thoughts captive and pondering seriously. 2 Corinthians 10:5 warns us to "take every thought captive," making them obedient to Christ. If we want to truly focus on what's important, we have to decide what in the world to do with this lack of love for ourselves and our present circumstances. We need to say no to the distraction of

161

detrimental daydreams and keep our hearts and minds focused on the Lord and what He has for us and our families. To discipline our thoughts and What if questions and replace them with God's truth – who He is, what He has done, and what He will do."
-Anne-Renee Gumley, Co-Author of Shiny Things

I remember the night I read these words. I remember the feeling when God revealed the sin I had been sitting in for years. I wanted to run and hide, but at that moment, His gentle rebuke pierced my heart. I was no longer hiding this part of me in the dark; now, it was in His light.

These thought patterns no longer had a grip on me the way they had for all those years. The daydreams, the "detailed memories" that sucked me in, and the discontentment that once held so much weight on me were finally in their rightful place, under the authority of God Almighty. God wants this for you, too. He calls us to "take every thought captive and make it obedient to Him" 2 Corinthians 10:5. He desires for us to "know the truth that sets us free" John 8:32 and to live out this freedom by handing over our thoughts and feelings to Him.

Hand over the discontentment, the daydreams, and the details of your past. Talk with a trusted friend or mentor as you lay these feelings at the foot of the cross. Be honest with the Lord about your struggles—He already knows them. You will begin to feel a shift in your heart when you go to Him, ready and willingly surrendered.

This week, lean into the conviction of what you aren't taking captive and making obedient to Christ. Journal, pray, and find scripture to set your mind on as you reshape your thought life to honor God.

Lord, thank you for loving me so much that you will do whatever it takes to reveal the sin in my life. Help me keep my eyes on you, thoughts on you, and a heart steadfastly pursuing what honors you. In Jesus' name, amen.

thoughts

THE SPIRIT OF TRUTH

"When the Spirit of truth comes, he will guide you into all the truth, for he will not speak on his own authority, but whatever he hears he will speak, and he will declare to you the things that are to come."
John 16:13

In the early days of my walk with the Lord, I remember wondering how we would know we're being deceived? I realized no one would walk around holding a sign that says, *I'm seeking to deceive you.* This deeply concerned me until I began unpacking what Jesus promised us in John 16:13. "When the Spirit of truth comes, he will guide you into all the truth, for he will not speak on his own authority, but whatever he hears he will speak, and he will declare to you the things that are to come." Friend, this is good news.

We in Christ have been gifted the Holy Spirit, which means the Holy Spirit lives in our hearts! Thank You, Lord! Because of this, we can trust that the Spirit will always lead us in truth, point us away from the errors of our flesh, as well as the deceptions of the world.

1 John 4:6 reminds us of this, too. "We are from God. Whoever knows God listens to us; whoever is not from God does not listen to us. By this, we know the Spirit of truth and the spirit of error." We will know the difference between the bearers of truth and the schemers by their willingness to uphold God's Word.

Galatians 5:25 tells us, "If we live by the Spirit, let us stay in step with the Spirit." From this, we know that those who live by God's unwavering truth will be in alignment with His truth.

These three pieces of Scripture alone give us clarity around this issue of desiring to understand how we will know if we're being deceived:

We will know by following the prompting of the Holy Spirit and
remembering the Holy Spirit only leads in truth.

We will know faithful followers of Christ by their acceptance
of the true Gospel.

We will know those who are in Christ by the reflection of their lives and
seeing the Spirit lead them.

Trusting that the Spirit will lead us in truth is also a call for us to trust God more deeply and intimately to know His Word. When we seek the heart of God, we see the leading of the Holy Spirit in our life. When we see the Holy Spirit leading in our life, we see the gift of discernment taking place and our continually deepening dependence on the Lord.

This week as you go out in the world, remember what Jesus said about the Holy Spirit, write John 16:13 on your heart, and trust His lead. Know fully that He will always lead you to the truth and away from error. The Spirit will never contradict the Word of God. Live this boldly for those around you and ask that the Lord allow you to share this with someone in your midst.

Lord, thank you for the gift of the Holy Spirit. I pray that I seek to obey where the Spirit leads and not turn from the protection it gives me. Father, I pray for a bold faith for you that knows your Word and desires to grow in discernment. As I go about my day, I ask that I be stirred up to be on fire for truth. I pray against the deception of the enemy and ask that error would be far from me. In Jesus' name, amen.

thoughts

THE CALL TO COMMUNITY

"And Jesus came and said to them, 'All authority in heaven
and on earth has been given to me. Go therefore and make
disciples of all nations, baptizing them in the name of the Father
and of the Son and of the Holy Spirit, teaching them to
observe all that I have commanded you. And behold,
I am with you always, to the end of the age.'"
Matthew 28:18-20

The call for us to be in community isn't a suggestion, it's something we must do out of obedience to the Lord. Our culture has challenged this way of living God's desires for those who follow Him.

This has had me thinking about examples from scripture that can lead us out of the complacency found in culture's way of relationships and press into the sometimes-difficult call to getting in community with a body of believers.

First, let's start in the garden with Adam and Eve. God saw that man needed a helper.

"But for Adam there was not found a helper fit for him. So the
LORD God caused a deep sleep to fall upon the man, and while he slept
took one of his ribs and closed up its place with flesh. And the rib that
the LORD God had taken from the man he made into a woman and
brought her to the man. Then the man said, 'This at last is bone of
my bones and flesh of my flesh; she shall be called Woman, because
she was taken out of Man.'" Genesis 2:20-23

Then let's look at Ruth and Naomi. These two women's lives exemplified the beauty of mentorship and relationships with multi-generation.

"But Ruth said, 'Do not urge me to leave you or to return from following
you. For where you go I will go, and where you lodge I will lodge. Your
people shall be my people, and your God my God. Where you die I will
die, and there will I be buried. May the LORD do so to me and more also if
anything but death parts me from you.' And when Naomi saw that she was
determined to go with her, she said no more." Ruth 1:16-18

Last, we must look at the Great Commission Jesus left with us. This alone concludes that we have to be in community to build relationships in order to train up disciples.

> "And Jesus came and said to them, "All authority in heaven and on earth has been given to me. Go therefore and make disciples of all nations, baptizing them in the name of the Father and of the Son and of the Holy Spirit, teaching them to observe all that I have commanded you. And behold, I am with you always, to the end of the age." Matthew 28:18-20

I know community can be an uncomfortable thing to commit to, but that doesn't mean we get to dismiss what we know we have to do. We have to trust where the Lord leads us and who He leads us to. We have to continue showing up knowing that these relationships knit by God will take time and intentionality.

Personally, walking in obedience to this command from the Lord has stretched me in ways I could've never imagined, but it has also blessed me beyond belief. Our Heavenly Father intentionally places us with people, and I've seen this faithfulness. The groups of women He has surrounded me with has been one of the greatest gifts of grace I've ever received.

I pray that you know God cares about where He places you. He's not going to lead you to a group of people without a purpose. I can promise you He has handpicked relationships that will sharpen you and challenge you. These people will not only love you, but point you to Jesus and His Great Commission.

Whether you're searching for a church home, Christ-centered friendships, or a Christian mentor, don't give into the temptation to dismiss the importance of this call. Trust the Lord, keep showing up, follow in obedience as He paves the way for you to be exactly where He wants you to be.

This week take time to write out prayers for those God has placed in your life, ask how you can be praying for them. If you're in the season of waiting for community, write a specific prayer for this desire and ask for an unwavering faith as you trust Him.

> Lord, help me trust you as I walk through this season of seeking community and to be open to accepting new people into my community. I pray to be a woman that values Godly relationships and has a heart that points everyone back to you. Lord, I ask for a mouth that speaks only goodness about the women I'm around, help me to turn from the temptation of gossip. Lord, I want to live a life that honors you and serves others, help me be the hands and feet in my community.
> In Jesus' name, amen.

thoughts

DESIRING GODLY FRIENDSHIPS

"Love one another with brotherly affection.
Outdo one another in showing honor."
Romans 12:10

Ten years ago, my parents and I loaded up all of my things and moved me to Columbus, Ohio. I'll never forget that day. It was the beginning of a new season, which meant the closing of many doors. I left behind most of the friendships I'd ever known and said goodbye to a life, I quite honestly, never wanted to go back to.

Brokenness plagued my relationships and choices. This new beginning ahead of me was so much more than just a move; it was the starting of the season in my life where I would find Christ and learn what genuine friendship really looked like.

I remember talking to the Lord often with my faith the size of a mustard seed in my little 650 square foot studio apartment, praying, "When will I meet *forever friends*?" I'd whisper. I look back over that season and see exactly what God was doing. He was drawing me closer to Himself, and He was teaching me to trust that He'd lead me to people who loved, honored, and served Him.

By God's grace, over the last ten years, He has shown me that I needed to walk through this season. He taught me what it looked like to love Him first and live expectantly as I trusted Him for the friendships He had for me.

This perspective changed everything for me, and I pray it does for you. That first, we must have our eyes set on the Lord and seek relationships that glorify and honor Him. Second, when we are waiting for godly friendships, we can trust that the Lord will bring people into our lives to help steward us, challenge us, and point us to Him.

Through my years of seeking godly friendships, I've learned that the heart of God isn't only seen within one friendship, the heart of God seen within a lifetime of different friendships. We get to see the unique characteristics and complexities of who God is through the hearts of His children.

The Lord kindly laid out the foundations of friendship through His Word. Romans 12:10-13 tells us not only how to live this out but also what to pray:

"Love one another with brotherly affection. Outdo one another in showing honor. Do not be slothful in zeal, be fervent in spirit, serve the Lord. Rejoice in hope, be patient in tribulation, be constant in prayer. Contribute to the needs of the saints and seek to show hospitality."

Having Romans 12:10-13 as the foundation for our relationships will certainly bear fruit in our lives. We also need to remember though that we are all fallen. We will misstep. We may even at times fail each other, and thankfully there is grace for that.

I pray this has encouraged your heart today, knowing that you can rest in God's faithfulness to lead you to Christ honoring friendships. Be attentive to His Spirit, stay the course when it gets difficult, and remember that His heart is for you!

This week, take a step back and evaluate the friendships in your life. Are they godly, do they point you to Christ, do they point you away from sin? Ask the Lord to lead you to women who seek to know God more deeply and want to walk alongside you as you too, grow in your relationship with Him.

Lord, I'm so thankful that you knit in us the deep desire for relationship. I pray as I seek godly friendships, I would keep an open mind for who you've picked to come alongside me. Older, younger, same season, or different, help me to trust that you know the best people for me. Help grow me into the type of friend who loves her people well and can point them to the truth. God, I trust you in this season as you grow my faith in this area of my life. In Jesus' name, amen.

thoughts

week forty one

CHEERING FOR HER ASSIGNMENT ...
(WHEN I HOPED IT WAS MINE)

"Not to us, O Lord, not to us, but to your
name give glory, for the sake of your steadfast
love and your faithfulness!"
Psalm 115:1

This title stings. It's not a fun topic to wrestle with and process. It reveals pride, entitlement, and the fleshly desire to "root for your people" only when you feel like it's not against the very thing you want. This looks different for all of us. For you, it might be the job you've prayed for, perhaps you're asking the Lord for a spouse, maybe you've had years of negative pregnancy tests, or the fact that life just doesn't look like what you hoped it would. This stings all the more when someone close to you seems to have all the "things" you hoped for and all the assignments you prayed for.

Oftentimes when we face seasons like this, it starts to take a toll on us spiritually (though we know it shouldn't) and it changes the way we approach God. Our hearts of thanksgiving are quickly turned to stone, our minds quickly shift to focusing on earthly things, and our once unshakable confidence seems like it's crumbling. But what if I told you that the crumbling of us and the derailing of our flesh's confidence is creating ground God can now move in?

Crumbled was exactly how I felt the day I received a text from a friend telling me a piece of her writing was going to be published in a book. Sadly, this wasn't the only time I'd felt this way, but it was this most recent sting that left a big question mark in my prayers with the Lord.

"Why not me?" I asked, with a heart puffed with pride and defeat *(which as we know—pride comes before the fall)*. When I asked God this question, He placed these two things on my heart, *All of life is for His glory*, and to the phrase my dad has said to me my whole life, "Why not her?".

This stirred up conviction deep within me. What if she is who God wants to use to reach someone very specifically that I couldn't? Or perhaps the Lord wanted me to get honest with Him so I'd be attentive to acknowledge the sin creeping into my

177

heart. Honestly, it's probably both. God will use her writing to bless someone, and God revealed my pride in its fullness. The way God moves is incomprehensible, and by His grace He uses all things to chisel us into His image.

Today, as you read this, maybe your heart feels weary, tired, and hopeless. I want to again remind you of what God has continually pointed me to: "Not to us, O Lord, not to us, but to your name give glory, for the sake of your steadfast love and your faithfulness!" Psalm 115:1 Yes, the Lord wants to bless us, but the Lord ultimately is at work to display His glory. So, whatever the Lord is doing in your life right now, trust Him.

The answered prayer for your friend and the "yes" my friend received is exactly what God wants for her. He didn't make a mistake. He didn't overlook you. He sees you, He sees your heart, He hears your prayers, and He loves you. He wants us to trust Him fully and seek Him for understanding. He wants to sanctify us completely as we grow in our relationship with Him. Don't bypass the handpicked assignments for your life by looking at everyone else's. This week, as you spend time in prayer, pray for your heart to soften and for your eyes to be open to the things God has called you to do. Journal about the blessings He's given you and how you've seen His hands move within the making of them.

Lord, I know you see me, but on days when it's hard, remind me I'm not overlooked. Remind me that everything in life is to glorify and honor you. Help me to be the woman who cheers on my friends even if they receive something I've been praying for. May I never forget that you're a God of abundance and without measure. In Jesus' name, amen.

He sees you - Genesis 16:13

He sees your heart - Psalm 26:2

He hears your prayers - 1 Peter 3:12

He loves you - Jeremiah 31:3

He wants you to trust Him—Proverbs 3:5

He desires you to seek your understanding in Him—Psalm 119:34

thoughts

I TRUST IN YOU

"In God whose word I praise, in God I trust;
I shall not be afraid.
What can flesh do to me?"
Psalm 56:4

I'm sure you've been in the seasons, like me, when your voice shakes as you tearfully tell the Lord, "I trust in you." All God asks of us is to trust and fully surrender to Him and let Him lead our lives. Shaky voice, sweaty palms, or full of faith, if we're following the Lord, we're on holy ground. We can't overlook how sacred this is. When we are living on a mission for the Kingdom, we're standing in His victory no matter what our situation looks like. This is good news.

Two Bible stories come to mind when I think of people standing on holy ground. The first being Joshua from the Old Testament. We see in Joshua 6 that he obeyed God in leading his people, the Israelites, to march around the walls of Jericho. Joshua's reverence for God birthed an unshakable boldness in faith. After hearing from the Lord, he said to his people in verses 7 and 8...

"And he said to the people, 'Go forward. March around the city and let the armed men pass on before the ark of the Lord.' And just as Joshua had commanded the people, the seven priests bearing the seven trumpets of rams' horns before the Lord went forward, blowing the trumpets, with the ark of the covenant of the Lord following them."

Joshua knew He was standing on holy ground, and when we obey God and trust Him, we, too, can confidently walk wherever He calls.

The second is David. He was the man after God's heart. Something that's always stood out to me during David's life was his constant pursuit of the Lord, even when his enemies were swarming him, and it looked like it'd be a defeat. He was steadfast and always abounding in the Lord. Read from Psalm 56:1-4 with me...

"Be gracious to me, O God, for man tramples on me; all day long an
attacker oppresses me; my enemies trample on me all day long, for many
attack me proudly. When I am afraid, I put my trust in you. In God,
whose word I praise, in God I trust; I shall not be afraid.
What can flesh do to me?"

David and Joshua knew the Lord was moving on their behalf because they
trusted in Him. A key takeaway is this: the only reason they trusted God was
because of their intentional relationship with their Heavenly Father. They knew
He would never step out of alignment with His character.

What a reminder this is for us, that no matter what attacks come our way, no
matter the hardships we're presented, or even the incredible opportunities God
has put before us; we can confidently trust Him.

We can trust in the workings of our Creator. We see them all throughout
Scripture and we understand that all things take place in His timing, under His
authority. We see this through Joshua's obedience and boldness. We see this
through the trust David had even in the midst of the cries of his heart. So, friend,
as we grow in our knowledge of the Lord, deepen our relationship with the Him,
our trust in His heart grows alongside it.

This week let us put our stake in His holy ground and not the fleeting things of
this world. As you spend time in prayer, bring to Him your need to trust Him more.
Spend time in His Word and study the life of these two men who followed the Lord
no matter what, write what stands out to you about their stories.

Lord, thank you for continuing to keep my heart out of complacency.
As I continue growing in my faith, help me see the places I need to
trust you more. Just like Joshua and David—bless me with a
conviction that honors you above all. In Jesus' name, amen.

thoughts

LET US GO

"When the angels went away from them into Heaven, the shepherds said to one another, 'Let us go over to Bethlehem and see this thing that has happened, which the Lord has made known to us.' And they went with haste and found Mary and Joseph, and the baby lying in a manger."

Luke 2:15-16

The Christmas season is a favorite time of year in our home. It's filled with sweet sentiments and a quiet that we don't experience often enough. For me, I love getting to sit in the season's stillness and soak up the incredible gift we celebrate; *Emmanuel, God with us.*

Luke 2 holds one of the most treasured, sacred stories in all of Scripture, Jesus's birth. Something that stirred in my heart that I had never noticed before was the Shepherd's response once the angle of the Lord appeared to them.

"'...Let us go...', ...and they went with haste..." vs 15-16

The shepherd's had not one ounce of hesitation in their hearts to go find w had been spoken to them. How amazing is that? They had full trust in kno that when they reached their destination, led by the Lord, they would find the He promised them. What an example this is to you and me of what walk obedience looks like.

This story sheds a lot of light on a question we all need to ask ourselves, " we hesitate to go when the Lord calls us?" I really believe we've over comp things. For us women, we oftentimes find that in order to "go" we first ne with a friend over a cup of coffee and process what we think God wants Not that it's wrong to share with friends or ask for prayer, but we've all "following the call" to weigh to heavily on the response of others. When the only response that should be happening is our "yes" to God.

This story of the shepherd's also points me to the incredible thing throughout His ministry. He moved when God called Him. He didn't he didn't take things to the crowd for approval. He took things out o to God, to the masses, and individual people whose lives were then pierced by the Gospel.

Going, doing, moving, and being on a mission for God ultimately boils down to reverence, deep trust, and obedience to Him. We can't lose sight of this. Obeying God means we don't hesitate or delay the call. This means instead of making the "call" about us and sharing it with everyone around us for approval, we must keep it focused on Him.

Friend, let us go... for God. Let us go with haste to share Him to the ends of the earth. Let us willingly serve where He has us and move without hesitation when He calls us. I pray we take our eyes off the way the world tells us to do things and start bringing it back to the heart of the gospel. Keep it focused on Jesus. Trust in the unchanging Word of God and remember the one who calls you, is with you.

This week, spend time studying Christ's first coming, look at the obedience of all involved in the story. Pray for a heart that serves Him the same, full of faith without hesitation.

Heavenly Father, thank you for your son, Jesus. Thank you for always showing us examples through your Word of how we should live for you. Lord, as I go out into the world this week, remind me that I am a walking ambassador of Christ, one who walks without hesitation as I get to live for you. I love you. In Jesus' name, amen.

thoughts

WE ARE HIS WORKMANSHIP

"You are fearfully and wonderfully made,
wonderful are his works. I know that full well."
Psalm 139:14

For years, I was plagued with feeling inadequate and insecure. One day I got in the car as tears fell down my cheeks. It was as if all the feelings of inadequacy and insecurity I'd ever felt landed in my lap all at once.

What I noticed most that day was that for so long, I truly believed that I was sufficient, that I could "be enough" if I thought good enough thoughts about myself. Wow, how wrong I had gotten it. You see, the Lord tells us in Psalm 139 that,

"You are fearfully and wonderfully made, wonderful are his works. I know it full well." Psalm 139:14

We are fearfully and wonderfully made. He didn't say, "you are enough". We in our flesh can't be; we are fallen, and we were the ones in need of saving. Don't you see the Lord doesn't tell us to be *enough*. He tells us to be surrendered. Why? Because we are His workmanship. Crafted and formed together by His hands.

Through the promise we have because of the cross, we can trust that God is sufficient in our weakness. When I think of weakness in the flesh, I think of Moses. He was the man God used to lead the Israelites out of exile and to the Promised Land. While Moses knew that he wasn't enough; he allowed his weakness to create doubt in God's call over his life.

God's call over Moses:

"Then, the Lord said, 'I have surely seen the affliction of my people who are in Egypt and have heard their cry because of their taskmasters. I know their sufferings, and I have come down to deliver them out of the hand of the Egyptians and to bring them up out of that land to a good and broad land, a land flowing with milk and honey, to the place of the Canaanites, the Hittites, the Amorites, the Perizzites, the Hivites, and the Jebusites. And now, behold, the cry of the people of Israel has come to me, and I have also seen the oppression with which the Egyptians oppress them. Come, I will send you to Pharaoh that you may bring my people, the children of Israel, out of Egypt.' But Moses said to God, 'Who am I that I should go to Pharaoh and bring the children of Israel out of Egypt?' He said, 'But I will be with you, and this shall be the sign for you, that I have sent you: when you have brought the people out of Egypt, you shall serve God on this mountain..'" Exodus 3:7-12

Moses' first response:

'But Moses said to the Lord, 'Oh, my Lord, I am not eloquent, either in the past or since you have spoken to your servant, but I am slow of speech and of tongue.' Then the Lord said to him, 'Who has made man's mouth? Who makes him mute, or deaf, or seeing, or blind? Is it not I, the Lord? Now therefore go, and I will be with your mouth and teach you what you shall speak.' But he said, 'Oh, my Lord, please send someone else.' Exodus 4:10-13

Often, you and I do the same thing. Like Moses, we allow our feelings of inadequacy, or our desire to falsely believe that we can be enough, trump what God really desires for us. In Psalm 139 and through Moses' life, we can see that all God wants for us is to remember that we are His workmanship, created for His purpose. We are fearfully and wonderfully made by Him, for Him!

Here we have full confirmation through God's Word that we will never be enough, we won't be sufficient, but we are covered by the One who is enough and abundantly sufficient. We have to hand over our insufficiencies, inadequacies, and insecurities to the Lord. Through that process, we will see His glory on display, making us whole in ways we never could.

Let us no longer allow the world or the enemy to fill our mouths and minds with our lacking, but bring them before the throne of grace as we seek to be made whole in Christ. Let us trust that as we live tethered to Him, He will pave the way for the plans He has for us.

This week, as you spend time with the Lord, ask Him to show you the parts of your life that you're striving to be "enough" in. Pray for a heart that desires to be used by Him, no matter what you think your lacking's are. As you process through this, dig into God's Word and see how the Lord is our all-sufficient sustainer.

Lord, thank you for your Word and promise that you are sufficient. As I journey through this life, remind me that I am not enough, and that is exactly how it should be. Lord, thank you for being the safest place for me to bring my inadequacies and insecurities. You are the greatest Father. In Jesus' name, amen.

thoughts

week forty five
WE ARE THE MESSENGERS

"Jesus said to her, 'I who speak
to you am He.'"
John 4:26

When I was a 19-year-old rebellious *hot mess*, the Lord met me in one of the most incredible ways. At this point in my life, I was becoming stunningly aware that I was at the end of my rope. Maybe you've been there, too? It was here that life began unraveling at the seams.

My life was filled with bad choices, hard consequences, and a heart filled with so much brokenness that I didn't think it could ever be made whole. But God. It was a beautiful Saturday morning when I woke up after very late night. I got in my car, headed home, and ten minutes later, I was standing next to my wrecked car that matched my very wrecked soul.

Between my sobs on the phone with my parents and the tow company, a woman in tattered clothes approached me and sat next to me on a small brick wall. She put her arm around me and looked at me with a heart full of compassion. She then asked me a question that changed my life and changed my heart forever: "Has anyone told you they loved you today?"

With uncontrollable tears flowing, I responded with, "Probably my mom."

She looked at me and said, "Well, God loves you every day. If you need anything, just call."

I remember looking behind me, so confused where she came from and how would I call her? The building behind me didn't seem like any type of housing and she didn't give me a phone number to call if I needed any more help. But I now know who sent her. The Lord sent her to meet me at my well. (John 4)

"A woman from Samaria came to draw water. Jesus said to her, 'Give me a drink.' (For his disciples had gone away into the city to buy food.) The Samaritan woman said to him, 'How is it that you, a Jew, ask for a

193

drink from me, a woman of Samaria?' (For Jews have no dealings with Samaritans.) Jesus answered her, 'If you knew the gift of God, and who it is that is saying to you, 'Give me a drink,' you would have asked him, and he would have given you living water.'" John 4:7-10

The way this woman approached me with truth and love changed my life forever. I soon gave my life to Christ after this took place. He used this moment that looked hopeless in my life as an opportunity to experience the gospel. Because of what happened that day, if I feel led to approach someone to pray, I almost always follow that prompting. If the Lord places someone on my heart to check in with, I do. I want to be a woman not only on a mission for God, but a woman who will boldly carry out the message (gospel) of the Lord.

The Lord doesn't call us to be His messengers so that we stay comfortable; instead, it's quite the opposite. Being a messenger for the Lord means we boldly declare His message throughout the earth and sometimes that can even be on the roadside.

"And Jesus came and said to them, 'All authority in heaven and on earth has been given to me. Go therefore and make disciples of all nations, baptizing them in the name of the Father and of the Son and of the Holy Spirit, teaching them to observe all that I have commanded you. And behold, I am with you always, to the end of the age.'" Matthew 28:18-20

I'm sure there is someone in your life right now that needs to hear the message of Christ. Or perhaps it's you who is wrestling with the truth that God absolutely, undeniably loves you and pursues you. Whichever one you find yourself relating to, spend time in prayer this week while looking at Scripture about God's pursuit of you and how He wants to use you to pursue others.

Heavenly Father, thank you for the moments you've sent us messengers. I praise you for pursuing me and saving me. I pray for a heart that I will always be willing to share the message of hope and redemption to whoever you put in my path. As I move forward this week, give me eyes to see people as you see them and ears willing to listen to someone who needs to know they are seen. In Jesus' name, amen.

thoughts

CELEBRATE, WE WILL!

"All Scripture is breathed out by God and profitable for teaching, for reproof, for correction, and for training in righteousness, that the man of God may be complete, equipped for every good work."
2 Timothy 3:16-17

I love picturing the life of Jesus, do you too? I love reading through Scripture and try imagine His birth, Him taking His first steps as a wobbly toddler. Him attentively sitting on the floor of the temple, soaking in the teachings from the Rabbi. I try to imagine watching Him walking up to be baptized by John, and what a miracle it would've been seeing Him feed the 5,000. Can you imagine getting to see these in the flesh? That's a gift I'd give just about anything to witness. And while that would be an amazing gift, to know we got to see Jesus during His earthly ministry, I am reminded that we have the greatest gift living on this side of the cross.

Being on this side of the cross means:

The Holy Spirit not only resides in you and me but leads us in truth; death has no more sting, and we have the written infallible Word of God.

"When the Spirit of truth comes, he will guide you into all the truth, for he will not speak on his own authority, but whatever he hears he will speak, and he will declare to you the things that are to come." John 16:13

"'O death, where is your victory? O death, where is your sting?' The sting of death is sin, and the power of sin is the law. But thanks be to God, who gives us the victory through our Lord Jesus Christ." 1 Corinthians 15:55-57

"All Scripture is breathed out by God and profitable for teaching, for reproof, for correction, and for training in righteousness, that the man of God may be complete, equipped for every good work." 2 Timothy 3:16-17

This leaves me in awe of all the undeserved gifts God has given us. This reminds me of the passage of Scripture that changed my life forever and is the reason you're holding this book.

John 3:30 declares, "He must increase, but I must decrease." These are seven life-changing, powerful words spoken by John the day Jesus was baptized. These seven words continue to remind me of the gift that Jesus and His life are to all of us. Because of Jesus and His life, we can live in a posture of decrease, so our lives increase in Him. How amazing is that?

Our Heavenly Father loved us so much that He sent His perfect, sinless son Jesus to come and take on the penalty of all we would ever do so we would have the opportunity to be made right with Him and live eternally together. This leaves me speechless. What a powerful, all-consuming redemption story this is, and it's offered to you and me. We have the choice to accept Christ, and all His life was, is, and is to come. When we accept this, we see that we are grafted in (Romans 11:11-24.)

Think about that, God the Father sent Jesus, His son, to cover us. Without one part of Jesus's life there would be no opportunity to have the gift of grace and mercy, there would be no defeated grave, and no redemption from sin.

John 3:30 reminds us of how important it is that we live our lives centered on Jesus and not on ourselves. This means we have to decrease. Jesus's life calls us to take up our cross and follow Him. It calls us to love Him more than anyone or anything and to always walk hand-in-hand with His spirit as we point others back to Him. This is good news. The Lord wants to make us look like Him as we serve others on behalf of Him. That is something to celebrate and celebrate, we will!

This week, pray for an opportunity to share something God has done in your life. It doesn't have to be something extravagant, but something that you know was from Him. Use this opportunity to sow the seed of the Good News we have in Christ!

Lord, thank you for who you are and sending your son Jesus so that we would be made right with you. Help us to see that the work on the cross is something we get to experience every single day. Thank you for the freedom we have in Christ and loving us when we deserved the penalty Jesus paid. Help me live a life that points people to this gift of eternal life today and every day. In Jesus' name, amen.

198

thoughts

PROTECT WHAT'S BEEN GIVEN TO YOU

"Guard the deposit entrusted to you."
1 Timothy 6:20

I love the boldness we see in Paul's letters to Timothy. He never shied away from sharing the truth of God's Word to please man; instead, he lived with a heart on fire for the mission of Christ. We know from Paul's writings that he had great joy and reverence in his heart as he trained up younger believers to know God and share the gospel. He understood what it cost for the grace he received and how important it was to share what the Lord had entrusted to him. While you and I aren't Paul, we should have this same boldness. Why? Because we've been given our God-given testimony, and with this, we can steward people's hearts to Christ.

This letter to Timothy stirred up conviction in my heart as I sat down one afternoon, wanting to take a breather from responsibility. *"Guard the deposit entrusted to you."* The Lord reminded me. I could no longer pass off the inventory God needed me to do in my heart. Was I doing what this Scripture said? Was I living out this call? No, I wasn't. I was serving some of my most sacred gifts from a place of depletion and not Christ's abundance.

This journey isn't about attaining the look of perfection but seeking to please God and live by His ways. So, this leads me to ask you this...

Who or what has God entrusted to you? What good thing is He asking you to guard or tend to? Are there people under your roof that you've been serving from a state of depletion? Has the Lord entrusted you with the assignment to love the neighbor down the street that may see things differently than you, or honestly, maybe it's your walk with Jesus and you've chosen to let the gift of that relationship take a seat on the bookshelf?

Whatever it is, do you sense the Lord stirring in your heart? Are you loving, leading, and living from a place of abundance in the Lord? While this will look different for all of us in the day-to-day, what should be the same across the board is that we make our time with God of utmost importance. We have to spend time with the Lord if we desire to love and guard those in our life well. When we don't, I can tell you firsthand what takes place. Selfishness and discontentment begin seeping into every facet of our days, and we miss the gifts God has placed right in front of us.

So, you may be asking yourself; how do I make time for the Lord, serve what's been entrusted to me, and make the time to lean into godly correction? Obediently show up. Give the Lord your middle minutes. Read His Word, listen to truth-filled worship music, and have an ongoing conversation with Him. Living this way will set up your heart to love, serve, and honor the deposits He's entrusted to you.

By making the Lord of utmost importance, we'll be serving from a place of abundance in Him, not the depletion of self. And this doesn't mean we won't be tired from time to time.

This week, spend time reading 1 and 2 Timothy. Pray for specific opportunities to share His love, truth, and grace with those He entrusted to you!

God, as I step out into the world help me to see each person as your Child. Created, loved, and bought with a price. Help me Lord, to take care of all the things you've entrusted to me. I pray as I dive deeper in living a life motivated by you and less of me that I will see you moving with much more clarity because my heart is more focused on you.
In Jesus' name, amen.

thoughts

DIVING DEEPER   Living With Less
podcast   *Episode #30*

GUARD YOUR EYES

"The eye is the lamp of the body.
So, if your eye is healthy, your whole body will be
full of light; but if your eye is bad, your whole body
will be full of darkness. If then the light in you
is darkness, how great is the darkness!"
Matthew 6:22-23

After years of praying for reasons why and how certain areas of sin and fear entered my life, God revealed that it wasn't something that was done to me or something I did, but something I saw. He led me to the place where the seed of destruction and curiosity were sewn. It was planted as a seven-year-old sitting at someone else's home exposed to something someone my age should never see.

Sadly, this still happens once we're adults. Somewhere along the way, the lie has been sown that just because we're adults means anything we want to see is permissible. "It's a movie, it's not real. It doesn't bother me, I'm not sensitive to that," are the excuses we use to allow ourselves to be exposed to garbage. God's Word tells us to be aware of this slippery slope.

"The eye is the lamp of the body. So, if your eye is healthy, your whole body will be full of light; but if your eye is bad, your whole body will be full of darkness. If then the light in you is darkness, how great is the darkness!"
Matthew 6:22-23

Need I say more? This statement made by Jesus in Matthew 6 makes it black and white. Yes, while conviction varies from person to person, light and darkness do not. What we take in through our eyes will absolutely affect our hearts, minds, and awareness of the Lord.

This also makes me think about those in our lives that are what I like to call the "onlookers". These are the people who have a front-row seat to watching how we live. We all have them. So, I want to pose this question to you that I've had to ask myself. What do you think happens when they watch us submerge ourselves in things that Christ calls us to refrain from? This caused deep conviction in my heart.

205

We are called to be the "salt of the earth, the light of the world, a city set on a hill that cannot be dimmed." (Matthew 5:14) This isn't to be taken lightly. This assignment will always cost us something. We can't live claiming Christ crucified yet look like the rest of the world. We must walk in wisdom with what we see, how we live, and what we are leading others to.

Think of it this way, guarding our eyes is not only going to be a blessing because it honors God, but it also protects those who look to us as an example. Going all the way back to those years of my childhood, the Lord never wanted me to see the things I did; but because of the lack of conviction and responsibility of the adults in charge, I was exposed. Had they been guarding their hearts and minds out of obedience to God, they would've been guarding mine too.

Let us be followers of Christ who choose to walk into conviction gladly because we know it's God doing His work in us. Let's remove the things that taint our minds and begin taking in the fruit that God desires for us. Join me this week as we ask the Spirit to lead us through the things we need to lay down at the cross and walk away from forever. Let us seek healing from our Healer and be redeemed from roots of bondage. Last, let us be women who lead others to truth and steward hearts towards godliness.

Lord, help me be a woman who keeps sacred what you call sacred. I pray my heart stands firm in your convictions and that I will choose to remove the things in my life that take my eyes off you. Give me eyes that seek to see what you're doing on behalf of The Kingdom. Lord, I repent of the things I've chosen to expose myself to and I ask that you restore that brokenness to wholeness. Lord, I ask that you remove the things from my mind that I was exposed to without asking, please restore the innocence that was taken from me in those experiences. In Jesus' name, amen.

thoughts

A WILLING HEART

"For God did not send his Son into
the word to condemn the world,
but to save the world through Him."
John 3:17

My husband and I recently watched The Case for Christ. All I have to say about that movie is, "WOW". This is a must watch for all Christians. While Lee Strobel set out to debunk Christianity, God met Him there. What stood out to me most apart from all the undeniable proof of the Lord, was the man in Lee's life that encouraged him to go on this "adventure". It's like he knew what the outcome would be because Christ will always be provable—you can't deny the history. All the Lord wanted was for Lee's heart to seek Him.

I've always looked at a willing heart as being something only a person who knows Jesus can have. But, as I watched this movie and saw the way God was meeting Strobel, I realized God will use any willingness directed towards Him to grab a person's attention. Whether they are believers or skeptics - God will use the willingness to captivate a wandering heart.

I know I've shared the story of Nicodemus before, but it rings so true again here. He, a legalistic Pharisee, had a willing heart to ask Jesus questions about the things he didn't understand. How often has my life looked like this? Even now, as a believer, I can wrestle with questions and delay taking them to the Lord. But then, in true Nicodemus fashion, nighttime comes, and I willingly cry out to God. It's a compelling picture when we think about it. As the darkness of the night sets in, we all go seeking the light.

How amazing is it that through Nicodemus's desire for better understanding came one of the most well-known pieces of Scripture? The one that shares why Jesus came, died, and had to rise again.

"For God so loved the world that he gave his one and only Son, that whoever believes in him shall not perish but have eternal life. For God did not send his Son into the world to condemn the world, but to save the world through him." John 3:16-17

Because of one willing man came one of the greatest messages shared by Jesus. It's incredibly powerful seeing that when Jesus shared this truth, it was not only for Nicodemus's heart but our hearts too.

The attributes of God's heart are endless. But one that never goes amiss is His willingness. This trait is knit into the heart of man because it stems from the heart of God, and God is always willing to meet one who desires to know Him. And in Lee Strobel's case He met his heart so intentionally that it became undeniable to him. Millions of people have read and watched The Case for Christ. It has pointed many of the viewers and readers into having a personal relationship with Jesus.

This week, as you spend time with the Lord, ask Him, "God, where do I need to be more willing in my walk with you? What part of my life have I not fully handed over that you want to bring a beautiful testimony out of?" Journal a specific prayer about desiring a willing heart and include all the Lord reveals to you.

Lord, help me have a willing heart. I pray for a spiritual awakening in areas of my life that I haven't fully handed over to you. Remove any unbelief that is keeping me from going deeper. Remind me that when I feel weary, all you ask for is my willingness to trust you.
In Jesus' name, amen.

thoughts

LIVING OUT THE TRUTH

"Jesus answered, 'I am the way and the
truth and the life. No one comes
to the father except through me.'"
John 14:6

Live your *truth*. It sounds simple, and free. This phrase struck my attention in 2019 when it became increasingly popular in America's culture, deeming it permissible to live in whatever form of "truth" you believed. This outlandish way of living and labeling nonsense as truth has now seemingly been ushered in by the falsehood of Progressive Christianity, Free Grace Theology, and Prosperity Gospel.

When thinking of this way of living I kept landing on the lives of the wandering Israelites and Samson. Both stories show their disobedience to God was due to them living in the "truths" they had been sinfully weaving in their hearts.

The Israelites blatantly showed they did not trust God. They continued to try to take matters into their own hands and put their truth above what God command of them. They were not only dismissive of God's provision, but they did not want to live within the timelines He had given them.

"This is what the Lord has commanded: 'Gather of it, each one of you, as much as he can eat. You shall each take an omer according to the number of the persons that each of you has in his tent.' And the people of Israel did so. They gathered, some more, some less. But when they measured it with an omer, whoever gathered much had nothing left over, and whoever gathered little had no lack. Each of them gathered as much as he could eat. And Moses said to them, 'Let no one leave any of it over till the morning.' But they did not listen to Moses. Some left part of it till the morning, and it bred worms and stank. And Moses was angry with them. Morning by morning they gathered it, each as much as he could eat; but when the sun grew hot, it melted." Exodus 16:16-20

We also must look at Samson, full of God's wisdom, who exchanged this gift to put his fleshly desires as a higher priority. He dismissed the truth for a life that ended up leaving him empty. He chased a truth that looked good, felt good, and somehow seemed good until it was not good. What Samson chose was apart from God, fleshly desired, and filled with consequences God never wanted for him. But, this is what *false* pride-filled, apart-from-God *truth* does.

> "When Delilah saw that he had told her all his heart, she sent and called the lords of the Philistines, saying, "Come up again, for he has told me all his heart." Then the lords of the Philistines came up to her and brought the money in their hands. She made him sleep on her knees. And she called a man and had him shave off the seven locks of his head. Then she began to torment him, and his strength left him. And she said, "The Philistines are upon you, Samson!" And he awoke from his sleep and said, "I will go out as at other times and shake myself free." But he did not know that the Lord had left him. And the Philistines seized him and gouged out his eyes and brought him down to Gaza and bound him with bronze shackles. And he ground at the mill in the prison. But the hair of his head began to grow again after it had been shaved." Joshua 16:18-22

We can all relate to both stories not the exact story; but the disobedience of living in the worlds twisted promise of *your truth*. Flirting and partaking in sin, choosing disobedience, and living in various forms of *false* truth, will always lead to painful consequences. This is a way of living we as Christ-followers should run from.

Praise God that we have the Word and this leading of the Holy Spirit. This gives us a safe place and a way of escape from this deranged way of thinking. By God's grace, we have the gift of discernment, wisdom, and clarity where you and I are called, commanded, and guided to live out His unwavering truth to the world. Jesus said in John 14:6, "I am the way, the truth, and the life." He is it. His truth is the only truth. End of story.

So, to my sister in Christ, I pray you join me in picking up our cross today and every day moving forward to live out the truth of Jesus Christ to this world. This week spend time with the Lord praying for ways you can be bolder for the Kingdom and safeguard your heart from falling into the lies of this world.

> *Lord Jesus, help us see your truth as the only truth. When our flesh pulls away, God draws us back with reminders of who you are and who you call us to be. Jesus, remind us each day that you are the way, you are the truth, and you are life. By your grace, we live freely in who you are, and may we always celebrate that and steward people to follow you.*
> *In Jesus' name, amen.*

thoughts

GOD IS TRUTH

"When the spirit of truth comes,
He will guide you into all truth."
John 16:13

This world is messy. It's loud, vigorous, and opinionated. It squanders truth and deems it excluding. It elevates falsehood and celebrates it as love. This takes me back to my life before I was walking with Christ. I craved the false stability of living for the world and by the world's standards of "truth." I ushered in opinions of anyone and freely welcomed desires to feed my flesh. Feelings and emotion-based responses formed truth in my life. But, by God's grace, He swiftly saved my soul from this path of destruction.

When I came to know Christ, I knew nothing more than the Lord's prayer and John 3:16. Honestly, it amazes me I hung on to any amount of truth through my years of rebellion. These small seeds planted in my heart as a child would soon be watered and flourish into a deep desire to pursue the truths of God and His heart. I no longer wanted to live in this emotional state of being tossed back and forth by my feelings. My soul craved the actual truth, the undeniable, unwavering steadiness of God.

As I grew in the knowledge of His Word, His truth pierced the harshest parts of my flesh. The promise of sanctification permeated areas of my life I didn't know needed tending. Suddenly the truth I found in Christ became my anchor and falsehood had to flee.

I often think of Jesus's prayer in John 17. Jesus was praying to our Heavenly Father on behalf of those who were believers, not for those of the world. He prayed that we, as believers, would be sanctified in the truth because his Word is truth (John 17:17). This has always been a favorite part of Scripture for me. Why? It boldly lays out who created truth and why we're called to walk in it. God is truth, and the truth from God sanctifies our sinful flesh.

I can promise you this, God is all truthful. In Him, we find everything we need. Through Him, we become the salt of the earth and the light of the world. Because of His love for us, we were gifted His Son, and through Christ's life, we've received the truth of the gospel which changed our lives on earth and our lives eternally forever.

This week spend time in prayer and ask the Lord what areas of His truth you shy away from. Are there specific reasons why you hold back from sharing the truth of God's Word? Journal what the Lord reveals to you.

Lord reveal in me the areas of your truth I shy away from. Lead me to places in your Word that remind me you are always truthful, and that truth came from you. As I live in this world and await my eternal life with you, stir up in me a heart that is obedient to share your truth. Thank you for your Son and for the constant pursuit of my heart.
In Jesus's name, amen.

thoughts

DIVING DEEPER Living With Less
podcast   Episode #60

HE MUST INCREASE,
I MUST DECREASE

"He must increase,
but I must decrease."
John 3:30

I'm not sure how it happened so quickly, but here we are. The end of 52 challenging, changing, and shaping weeks where I pray you've grown in your hunger for God's Word and making Him the center of your life. Writing this brings so many emotions to my heart, because it's the ending to one of the most beautiful things God has done in my heart. The assignment was never taken lightly, and one that I am eternally thankful for.

When the Lord placed John 3:30 on my heart, I couldn't have imagined what He would do with that. But I was often reminded that when He leads, we need to follow. He lays things on our hearts, weaves things into our stories, and sets things into motion that we could never imagine.

"He must increase, but I must decrease." became the most healing, convicting, and challenging words of my life. They caused me to learn more about the heart of God and the desperate heart of man. It caused me to lean in, listen, and follow where the Spirit was leading. God used this passage to strip me of pride, division, and lack of trust. He used this to bring my heart to seeing the magnitude of the me-centered world we live in and that we are called to be Christ-centered no matter what.

As you walk through your days prayerfully asking God for wisdom, direction, and protection, remember that *we must decrease* for the Lord be on the throne of our heart. We cannot sidestep that. We can't share the throne of our life with anything or anyone else. He is it. He is Lord. I pray that your heart clings to living out John 3:30 as you watch Him continue to reveal the very things that get in the way of what He desires for you. Stay steadfast in your pursuit of Him and stay attentive to conviction, which leads to repentance.

It has been my joy and honor to walk alongside you this year. Know that I am praying for you. Know that God sees you, hears you, and desires to speak to you as you attentively seek Him through His Word. Know that He wants to be first in your life and have your whole heart. He will do what it takes to bring you to that place of surrender. He will love you, lead you, and teach you about His heart. My sister in Christ, I can't wait to one day meet you so that we can celebrate together as we talk about all the beautiful ways our lives increased in Christ as we decreased what got in the way of Him.

Lord, help me today to fully accept the truth of John 3:30. Make me aware of the things that are in the way of you. Awaken my spirit if it falls asleep and falls back into old patterns. Lord, remind me that you see me, you speak to me, and you pursue me daily. Thank you for always nudging me to know you more. In Jesus's name, amen.

thoughts

Lord - thank you for this sister in Christ. Thank you for her heart and her desire to know you more deeply. God, I pray you continue to lead her as she lives a life more for you and less for herself. Cover her with your protection and draw her near.
In Jesus' name, amen.

LIVING WITH LESS
podcast

LIVING WITH LESS
podcast

ACKNOWLEDGMENTS

Corey, Cam, and Collins Grace–
To the greatest blessings in my life, I love you and it is an honor to serve you! Corey, I praise God that I get to be your wife, and it has been a blessing to see how the Lord has used this ministry to not only grow me but grow us as one. Thank you for choosing to lead our family, fight for us, and leave me sweet notes with my coffee after late nights of writing! I love you! Cam, being your mom, has been the most rewarding and sanctifying journey. I've learned so much about the heart of the Father by getting to watch my love for you unfold in motherhood. You, my boy, are an answered prayer and a gift to all who know you. I love you! Collins Grace, what a gift it has been to carry you in my womb through this entire process. God is faithful and answered our prayers by giving us you! The Lord has used you daily to remind me of all the beautiful things He knits together in the unseen. I love you!

Mom and Dad–
The two greatest cheerleaders God could have given me. Thank you for believing in me, praying for me, disciplining me, and loving me through my highest highs and lowest lows. Your fingerprints and prayers are woven all throughout these pages. I love you!

To my prayer warriors–
Mary, from my first bible study teacher to trusted friend, thank you for always pointing me to Jesus. You've always been in my corner, challenged me, and pushed me to write for Jesus. Thank you for everything through the years! Paige and Shelly, you two have blessed me so much in this process. Thank you for reminding and encouraging me on the hard days to celebrate every little thing! Tabitha, Rachael, Alysha, Sarah, and Diane, thank you for being my girls to process with through this entire book writing journey! Diana, thank you for believing in this message and being my publisher. It is an honor to link arms with you and share it with the world! To God be the glory!!

TO ALL THE OTHERS WHO I WISH I COULD LIST

thank you

Thank you for the prayers and for believing me.
There are many fingerprints and prayers woven through
the pages of this book and I pray you see this as
God's faithfulness for the work He has done.

CPSIA information can be obtained
at www.ICGtesting.com
Printed in the USA
LVHW021112270523
748244LV00039B/789